Genius Mental Models:

Lessons From History's Greatest Minds on Innovation, Achievement, Creativity, and Intelligence

By Peter Hollins,
Author and Researcher at
<u>petehollins.com</u>

Table of Contents

CHAPTER 1: WHAT MAKES A GENIUS?   7

GENIUS AND INTELLECTUAL CURIOSITY   8
GENIUS AND HARD WORK   12
GENIUS AND INTELLECTUAL HONESTY   16
GENIUS AND POLYMATHY   19

CHAPTER 2: MOZART AND THE EMPTY PITCHER   29

THE CREATIVE PROCESS CAN'T BE HELD TOO TIGHTLY   31
USE THE "MOZART METHOD" IN YOUR OWN LIFE   32
POUR OUT. FILL UP AGAIN. REPEAT.   35

CHAPTER 3: EINSTEIN AND COMBINATORIAL PLAY   39

EINSTEIN: NOT A ONE-TRICK PONY   40
THE POWER OF THE POSSIBLE   44
EINSTEIN'S STRENGTHS   47

CHAPTER 4: BE PROLIFICALLY PRODUCTIVE LIKE PICASSO   53

RECONSIDER YOUR ATTITUDE TO "WORK"   55
EMBRACE EXPONENTIAL ACTION   57

CREATE A CONDUCIVE ENVIRONMENT 59

CHAPTER 5: SOCRATES' ENDLESS QUESTIONS 63

UNDERSTANDING THE SPIRIT OF THE SOCRATIC METHOD 65
APPLIED CURIOSITY 67
THE SOCRATIC METHOD IS A THINKING TECHNIQUE 73
TURNING THE QUESTIONS ON OURSELVES 75

CHAPTER 6: SUN TZU AND THINKING LIKE A WARRIOR 81

ENSURE APPROPRIATE ACTION 84
SEE THE WORLD THROUGH YOUR OPPONENT'S EYES 85
MASTER "PERSPECTIVE-SWITCHING" 87
THINK HOLISTICALLY 88

CHAPTER 7: DARWIN'S GOLDEN RULE 91

DARWIN'S UNCOMMON TALENT 92
TRUTH > BEING RIGHT 94
CONSISTENCY IS OFTEN MORE VALUABLE THAN BRILLIANCE 98

CHAPTER 8: MARIE CURIE AND THE IMPORTANCE OF TAKING RISKS 102

Embrace the Unknown	103
Take a Gamble on Yourself	105
Collaborate with Others	107

CHAPTER 9: RENE DESCARTES AND STARTING "FROM ZERO" — 113

Starting From Zero	114
Meditation 1	118
Meditation 2	123
Meditation 3	126
Descartes the Man	130

CHAPTER 10: TESLA AND EDISON: TWO PATHS TO SUCCESS — 137

Edison – A Teacher and Rival	138
Tesla's Lesson: Pursue Goals Obliquely	140
Edison's Lesson: Pursue Goals Incrementally	143
Two Very Different Kinds of Genius	148

CHAPTER 11: COPERNICUS AND GALILEO: THE COURAGE TO GO AGAINST THE GRAIN — 153

What It Takes to Be Different	154
Geniuses Are Leaders, Not Followers	157
Navigating Rejection	159

RESIST DETERMINISM	**161**
OWN YOUR WORK	**163**
HAVE FAITH IN YOURSELF	**164**

CHAPTER 12: ALAN TURING AND THE POWER OF NEGATIVE THINKING — 169

COMPUTING THE UNCOMPUTABLE	**172**
DON'T BE AFRAID OF UNSOLVABLE PROBLEMS	**173**
USE CONSTRAINTS AND LIMITS TO YOUR OWN PURPOSE	**174**
DEFINE SUCCESS BY WHAT IT ISN'T	**175**

CHAPTER 13: ABRAHAM LINCOLN AND HIS TEAM OF RIVALS — 179

"KEEP YOUR ENEMIES CLOSE"	**181**
MANY WAYS TO BE A GENIUS	**184**
THE POWER OF MINDSET	**186**
THE SECRET INGREDIENT: HUMANITY	**190**

Chapter 1: What Makes a Genius?

What is a genius? Perhaps the first thing that pops into your mind is the popular depiction of geniuses in TV shows. You know the kind: smart talking, slightly arrogant black sheep types who seem to solve the crime or win the chess tournament without breaking a sweat. People have always been fascinated with genius, and with the ability to wield superior intellectual mastery. Whether we admire geniuses in the arts, science, or business, there's something so irresistible about the idea of a human being operating at their fullest human potential.

If you've picked up this book, it's likely you too are interested in what exactly sets geniuses apart. Are they just born that way, and us mere mortals can do nothing but look on in admiration? Or perhaps there is no such thing as genius at all, only years of punishing, diligent hard work that pays off eventually?

In this book, we're going to take the perspective so often taken by geniuses themselves: we're going to approach the idea of intellectual mastery and success as our topic, and study it as Einstein studied physics. In other words, we'll become students of human success, and look closely not into any one subject, but into the way we think about those subjects, and how we can optimize. We'll observe, take notes, and see what we can learn from the great thinkers of our time – and there's a lot to learn, for those who are willing to pay attention.

What genius can you think of, off the top of your head? In this book, we'll look at the lives and works of people like Socrates, Einstein, Descartes, Darwin and Copernicus, among others. Despite living in different cultural and historical periods, and despite having different interests and ideas, these people in fact share a surprisingly predictable set of personal characteristics. So, what are these traits? Before you carry on reading, close this book and see if you can zoom in on just one or two qualities or attributes that you think make the essence of a genius.

Genius and intellectual curiosity
Chances are, you thought of something along the lines of "a genius is intellectually hungry and curious about everything." No matter the chosen outlet, intelligent and highly conscious people tend to want to know *why*. It's this active,

deliberate perspective that sets them apart from people who are happy to take things as they are, without ever looking more deeply into them.

When we are children, we are perhaps more like natural geniuses than at any other time in our lives. We are the proverbial learning sponges, soaking everything up, asking a million questions a day, wanting to know how things work just for the joy of having that knowledge. When we grow up, adults around us indoctrinate us into certain educational conventions and institutions that dull this natural curiosity. We learn the rules, the right answers, and which authority to defer to. In other words, we stop relying on our own innate fascination with the universe around us.

For a genius, the curiosity never seems to subside. No matter how old they are, they seem to have a knack of looking at the world with the wonder of a little child seeing it all for the first time. They are enraptured by things that other people think are commonplace. They want to understand how it all works, what it means, how it fits together, and they don't stop investigating until they find out!

Granted, many people in the world are dogged in their pursuit of knowledge. Picture a journalist relentlessly pursuing the "truth" or the next scoop, or an academic going over their field with a fine-tooth comb as they compile a PhD thesis. The difference here, though, is that such people may be pursuing knowledge and intellectual mastery for some secondary gain. For example, they are choosing to learn and develop skill so they can make money, or win the esteem of their peers, or satisfy the expectations of others. The genius, on the other hand, doesn't care about these things, or, at the very least, these gains are a distant second to the main reason for learning: "just because."

A genius pursues knowledge and understanding for its own sake. The thrill of learning, of peering into the mysteries of life, of gaining a grasp of what was once unintelligible to you – these things are seen as rewards in themselves, and they are their own good worth chasing. You can see this in the fact that many geniuses will pursue knowledge and understanding despite the fact that it actually compromises other things in life like money, security, and social approval. As we'll soon see, many of the most celebrated geniuses throughout history were actually reviled by their peers at the time, or sacrificed relationships and financial security in order to pursue the object of their intellectual fascination.

Geniuses are never lukewarm about the unknown, and they certainly don't fear it. Rather, they are enchanted with it, and seek to satisfy their curiosity. Their attitude is one of the natural scientist – they want to engage with the deeper functioning of the universal machine, rather than simply accept the surface manifestations.

Is this a trait that you can actually develop in yourself, though? Absolutely. Remember, we are all born with an innate curiosity – we wouldn't know what we know now or indeed have survived unless we were 100% fine-tuned natural learning machines! It's a question of reconnecting with that inborn curiosity and yearning to understand.

This attitude is one and the same with being "open-minded." Just for today, go out into the world and literally imagine that you are a child again and everything is new to you (or maybe imagine that you are an alien who is seeing Earth for the first time and trying to make sense of it). Spend a day asking questions of the things that are happening around you. Notice where your own curiosity is piqued. Where do you feel that rush of excitement and energy, that feeling that is as exhilarating as discovering a chocolate bunny on an Easter egg hunt?

When you notice yourself feeling this, pay attention. Go more deeply into the questions you have. Think creatively about what you see, and ask yourself, "in what ways could this be different?" Many geniuses are able to make enormous breakthroughs in their field precisely because they were able to see the profoundly obvious facts of existence that everyone else has dutifully trained themselves out of noticing.

Look for problems, and daydream about novel solutions to them.

We tend to think of geniuses as serious, joyless people, but nothing could be further from the truth. The start of every marvelous idea or innovation is essentially *play*. To access this state of mind, ironically, asks us to drop our ideas of being smart, of being right or admired by others. It asks us to forget about the *goals* we might attach to being intellectually superior. Many of the world's greatest discoveries are made by accident, when people relaxed their minds and simply looked at the same old things in a slightly different way.

We'll explore the fundamental value of curiosity, open-mindedness and a perspective of goalless play in subsequent chapters, but for now, imagine that a genius is nothing more than a child who sees the entire world as a vast and wonderful playground – with this mindset, you are halfway to being a genius yourself.

Genius and hard work
Of course, it's not all just fun and games. Though many *Eureka* moments have happened in the ways described above, this is only the start of the journey. A person who is blessed with loads of natural curiosity will find plenty of interesting avenues of enquiry to go down, but may never actually muster the energy and discipline to go all the way in any single one of them. This is

because another quality is essential for reaching that level we associate with genius: hard work.

If creativity, inspiration and curiosity are the spark that get the fire started, then at some point you need a constant source of fuel to keep those flames burning for the long term. When we look at geniuses or ultra-successful people, we only see their success. We see them at the end of their journey, once the grand theory has been pieced together, the invention finally works, or the magnum opus is finally completed.

But this is just the surface gloss, just a fraction of a percent of the total work that such a person has actually undertaken over years, often decades. This is like watching a person step over the finish line in a marathon – the final step is just one of hundreds of thousands of other steps that have brought them to that point, none of them quite as exciting as that last one!

Geniuses do the work that other people are not willing to do. These are the people who are prepared to stay up late into the night. In fact, it's insatiable curiosity *together with* relentless hard work that produce most of the genius's success. Without passion, they cannot push through challenge and adversity. Without the hard work, the passion is never attained and made real. People can become fatigued with their life course because although they have the fuel (i.e. the willingness to work hard) they lack the sincere love for the topic that helps "ignite" them. They give up long before the person who is willing to work hard, but also genuinely passionate about their path of action.

Patience, dedication and self-discipline are what's needed to *shape and direct* our natural and spontaneous intellectual curiosity. Like scientists, we need to organize and structure our inquiry into the world around us. Experiments of any kind are useless if they're not properly planned, logically laid out and diligently executed, often many, many times over. For this, we need to apply consistent effort and focus.

When you are driven by the "big picture" and are enjoying the process of learning for its own sake, you are able to defer the enjoyment that comes with success. You are able to wait for the payoff, sometimes for years, because you understand the process you're in. Patience and delayed gratification come easier when you are on a path you genuinely care about. If only money or praise are driving you, you will drop out of the race when it looks like the adversity is more trouble than it's worth. Or else, you may be tempted to settle for a smaller goal in the interim and forego the bigger prize because you want the satisfaction of achievement now rather than later.

So, a genius is a rare creature because they contain within them a powerful blend of two quite opposing forces: on the one hand, they are open minded, passionate, independent thinkers who pursue learning for the love of learning. On the other hand, they are supremely disciplined, focused and detail oriented, and can sit for a long time on work that may seem tedious and pointless to others, who cannot see the vision the genius is diligently working towards.

How can you cultivate this diligence in yourself? This is the realm of self-discipline. The genius is their own teacher, and they don't wait for external incentives to work hard. They just do it, and they keep doing it until they satisfy their own high standards. Then they up the standards! One way to bring some of this focus into your own life is to cut down on "noise" so you can better focus on the one (or maybe two) areas of life that are most important.

You might decide that each day, you only focus on one main task. Really get stuck into it, and tune out all distractions. Go deep into the work, beyond the superficial. If you're not challenged enough, push yourself more. If the work seems too hard, break it down and tick of smaller tasks until you gather momentum again. Whatever you do, don't accept anything other than movement on your task. You can move slowly some days and more quickly on others, but never allow a day to go by where you don't do something towards your chosen goal.

This attitude that sees work as non-negotiable will make it easier to get into good habits. We'll explore these techniques in greater detail later in the book, but a few fundamental principles underlie the most effective approaches. For example, set your grand goal... and then forget about it. Instead, turn your focus onto manageable, daily habits. Make work on your path seem as automatic as brushing your teeth every day. The big goals are achieved step by step – and the genius knows how to focus on those small, incremental steps. At the end of every day, they have moved forward, even if it's only a tiny amount.

Genius and intellectual honesty
Let's consider some other key traits. Imagine the genius at work, day after day. They try plan A, and it doesn't quite work. They tweak it and try another version, Plan B. This is better but still not quite right. They admit that some assumptions are not exactly founded. Plan C doesn't work at all, so they go back to the drawing board and begin afresh, this time with a completely new approach. And so on.

This kind of grueling step by step process requires patience and hard work, but it also needs something very important: humility. A person who is never willing to admit that they're wrong stops at the very first hurdle. If you are stubborn, have a big ego and hate making mistakes, you will stay precisely where you are, knowledge-wise. Those who close their eyes to evidence staring them right in the face are the *opposite* of scientists (and, in fact, they are the opposite of geniuses, you can pick your favorite description...)

As an extension of being playful, open minded and curious, one must have a sense of being willing to be led by the process of learning. Sometimes, this means that the process tells you, in no uncertain terms, "That's wrong! Try again." A genius takes this "negative" feedback for what it is, thinks, "hmm, that's interesting," changes their approach and simply tries again. A less-than-genius person looks at this feedback from the universe and is mortified. Because they have their ego wrapped up in the learning process, they see being wrong as a personal failure, and a reflection on who they are as people.

So, when they get things wrong, they feel that *they* are wrong, and understandably, this feels like a pretty serious threat. The response is to deny that they are wrong, ignore the evidence, or sit tight and never grow because it's too embarrassing to feel like a beginner. This is essentially the difference between a fixed mindset (i.e. "I am the way I am, and I can't change") vs. a growth mindset ("It's always possible for me to learn").

We can call this trait intellectual honesty. It's the ability to be flexible, to be honest with yourself and to self-correct without too much bias or stubbornness. The degree of your willingness to be wrong is directly proportional to your capacity to learn. After all, those who already know everything have no need to ask questions, to be better, or learn from others. So, they don't.

This is a trait that is very easy to develop in yourself, thankfully. How? It's simple: be embarrassed occasionally. One thing that is incredibly freeing for the soul and the intellect is to quickly say, "I don't know" when you really don't know. If you're in a discussion with someone who has just proven you incorrect, don't dig yourself further into a hole by doubling down on your position or trying to make it out that you were really right all along. Instead, say freely and quickly, "yes, I think you're right actually!" and simply let go of the idea or belief you held before.

Easier said than done. But if you can consistently practice this, you will soon develop intellectual honesty and ironically, people will view you and your opinions more favorably. You demonstrate not only intellectual maturity but wisdom and level-headedness when you can honestly admit gaps in your understanding. Remind yourself that being wrong or making mistakes is not the end of the world. In fact, if you're not regularly encountering your own ignorance and lack of skill, you aren't challenging yourself enough!

See mistakes and being wrong as the entry fee for playing the learning game. Remember that even brilliantly accomplished geniuses throughout history have been wrong – in fact, they've probably been wrong more times than you! The successful entrepreneur, it's said, has failed more times than the average person has even tried. The genius, then, is not someone who finds everything easy and gets it right first time; rather, they are the people who have a higher than normal threshold for tolerating uncertainty, "failure" or confusion.

They are the ones wiling to be embarrassing novices for years before they get to show off their skill. They are the ones who won't mind when people laugh at their crazy idea. While everyone else might feel sorry for a person who lost tons of money on a venture that didn't pan out, that person may themselves be thinking, "excellent! Now I know exactly what *not* to do next time. This is great…"

Other than regularly saying "I don't know" or "I was wrong" (and meaning it) the genius mindset is characterized by a sincere lack of bias and prejudice. Keep in mind your natural curiosity – it's not something that thrives in the presence of dogged beliefs and ideas that never budge. Take a look at your own self talk and see if you can identify any times where you use words like "always" and "never." These could give you a clue to your own stubborn biases or assumptions that may need updating.

Genius and polymathy
Let's move on to another fundamental trait, one which we can only call "jack-of-all-tradesness."

Genius thinking is more lateral than vertical. In other words, it's broad. Though geniuses like to look into things in depth, they are never specialists. This is because their natural curiosity carries them into all fields and topics. If you ask "why?" often enough, you will soon find yourself studying *everything* in life – and why not? Why restrict yourself?

As you'll soon see, the intellectual heavyweights of history all had this in common: they read widely, and had an enormous range of interests. If they were scientists, they dabbled in all kinds of science, and also enjoyed poetry, hunting, and economic theory (for example). If they were into politics they also had a religious interest and painted, or if they were philosophers, they also had a keen interest in anthropology and music. You get the idea. They didn't box themselves in. It's only the human mind that divides the world into little categories – geniuses see that everything is actually connected, and don't put limits on their inquiries.

A genius is well-read and up to date. They want to understand what is happening around them. So, when they talk to anyone, chances are they have something to contribute to the conversation, and if they are completely oblivious, they go into investigation mode and learn as much as they can when they encounter someone who knows something they don't. If they are familiar with mathematics and programming, and they chat to an expert in literature, they can't help but draw connections and relationships, seeking to understand the new knowledge in terms of the knowledge they already have. They might become curious about symbolic representation in literature, or wonder how an AI would codify and represent different writing styles, or how certain languages might be considered more "mathematical" than others.

In fact, it's this willingness to cross-pollinate different areas of knowledge that allows geniuses to come up with so many novel approaches and theories. Genius thinkers are at home with using analogies of all kinds. Their minds are constantly looking for the biggest possible picture. They want to know how everything fits together, so when they meet a new piece of knowledge, the first thing they do is examine it and see how it relates to the pieces they already possess. This is perhaps why so many truly great scientists are also deeply creative and artistic people – they know how to work with metaphor and analogy, and can rearrange concepts, switch perspectives, and "translate" ideas from one field to another.

The way to foster this trait in yourself is to deliberately seek out connections and interrelations in everything you do. Don't think in neat little boxes, but blend it all together. As a fun practice, look around in your life right now and identify one area in which you are an expert (or aspiring to be!). Now think of an area that you are quite ignorant of. Next, see if you can try to draw connections between them. Can you see how economies are a little like ecosystems? Or can you see how composing a complex orchestral piece is a bit like putting together a recipe? Maybe you can hear some music and imagine that it has its own vocabulary and language – or indeed that it can be understood as a kind of animal.

The point of making connections and relationships this way is not to discover any real or true links, but rather to open up your own horizons and start to see the world more broadly (i.e. as it really is!). Sadly, people are taught that "left brain and right brain" are different, and that people who are good at "hard" sciences will naturally be deficient in art and languages, and that those who are more creative and socially minded will flounder when it comes to things like business or engineering. A genius doesn't follow these rules in the least – remember, they see the world as a playground, and not as a house with rooms they're not allowed to go into.

In your own life, you can make a point of getting into the habit of never assuming something is outside your scope. Even if you think a certain topic or idea is too difficult or irrelevant, take a closer look anyway and see what you can learn.

Another good practice is to routinely court information from all parts of the spectrum, i.e. don't always go looking for material that only confirms the beliefs you already have. Don't assume you know what "the other side" think and believe – go and check it out yourself!

Get into real, good-faith arguments with people you disagree with and genuinely put yourself in their shoes. Deliberately seek out information online that contradicts your perspective, and see what happens. Besides saying "I don't know" more regularly than others, geniuses also say something else: "this is my opinion... for now. But it's only provisional. I'm willing to change it when I'm faced with evidence to the contrary."

Finally, in mentioning how geniuses are comfortable with holding provisional opinions and changing their minds when necessary, we can't help but consider something else about them, namely that they are seldom conventional people. Geniuses are constantly thinking outside of the box, or looking closely at the box itself to see what it's made of, and how it functions, and why. Such people are not rebels exactly, rather they follow their own principles, and seldom have blind respect for arbitrary rules they see no sense behind.

This is because they look more deeply into matters than is common; the world seems far more malleable and up for debate than it might seem to others – rules, in this case, can look like pointless limits and interference. We've already seen that the genius perspective is one that draws creative connections, sees hidden relationships, and investigates deeply into the real causes of phenomena. Things like baseless public opinion, random rules for the sake of rules, and fearfully towing the line are likely to be far from a genius's mind. But again, it's not as though the people we call genius get a thrill from rule breaking; it's more that they recognize a higher authority, and if they do end up obeying and following orders, it will be because they accept the validity of another deep thinker's perspective.

Genius thinking is more characterized by non-hierarchical social structures, non-linear thinking and a tendency to go against the grain – if the grain is something that is done merely by tradition and convention, rather than because it is genuinely the best way to do things. This is why geniuses are so often associated with science and innovation – these are the people who pull humanity forward with their insistence that there has to be more to life than there currently is, even if people are afraid of trying something new.

Genius thinking is dynamic and adaptable. It's not afraid to adjust itself, or to change as needed. Thus, a genius thinker will have no qualms about completely dropping an old way of life to pursue an entirely new way of being. They are happy to dream up novel solutions, creative new possibilities, or even fantastical and outlandish dreams for the future. They don't tend to take these thoughts and measure them against the accepted standards of the day. In other words, they don't care about being popular or fashionable or even liked by others. And this is what allows them to be true explorers of the unknown.

This can be a difficult perspective shift to bring into your own life, because every one of us, whether we admit it or not, is deeply embedded in the assumptions and rules of our culture and historical period. We all have our assumptions and biases, and our beliefs about what is and isn't possible, what's right and what's wrong.

One of the genius's best tools is the mindset that comes with asking, "what if?" and being genuinely open to whatever answers stem from that. Question your own "rules" that you make for yourself and you'll become better at recognizing the unnecessary limits placed on you by others. You could practice this mindset switching for yourself, right now. Get out a piece of paper and, very quickly and without too much thought, write down 5 things that you absolutely know to be true about yourself or the world. Write down your core beliefs or assumptions, big or small.

Let's say you wrote down, "I value education and learning so I'm going try to get into university."

Now, look at this as neutrally as you possibly can. Look at the unspoken conditional nature of the sentence, i.e. the assumption that going to university is the best (or only?) way to get an education. Consider the hidden biases and expectations behind this – that teaching and learning come from recognized institutions, i.e. from externally, and if you value education and learning you need to appeal to them to let them allow you to learn. It's just a simple sentence that you may never look more deeply into, but on closer examination, can you see how many rules are implied in it?

Maybe it's *not* true that university = education. A genius doesn't take anything for granted... they don't even take their own word for it. They ask, "what if...?" What if it were possible to learn more outside of university? What if the thing that you most wanted is actually not to follow the path that other people in your peer group are following?

The answers are irrelevant – it's the fact of asking the question that is important.

In the chapters that follow, we'll be looking more closely at specific examples of people who many have called genius. We'll see not only that each of these people has perfectly demonstrated the traits we've discussed here, but exactly how they managed to express these tendencies and traits in their work, and indeed how these characteristics were actually the key to their success.

Summary:

- Geniuses come in all shapes and sizes, and come from all walks of life and all historical periods, but they can all be seen to possess certain predictable characteristics and mindsets.
- If we can model our own lives on the traits we find in great and successful thinkers, we too can learn to fulfil more of our intellectual and creative potential.
- The first trait is a **lust for learning and an insatiable curiosity** about how the world works, and why. This is knowledge and understanding pursued for its own sake, and not because it indirectly leads to another goal like fame or money. Such inspiration and passion gives incredible stamina to any effort.
- Another trait is diligence, patience, dedication and self-discipline, i.e. everything associated with consistent **hard work**. Without detail-oriented and practical action taken daily, and a willingness to delay gratification, success will never materialize.
- **Intellectual honesty** is also important, and this includes humility and the ability to own that you don't know something, or that you have made a mistake. Geniuses know that

stubbornness, bias, expectation and ego can undermine genuine learning.
- Most genius types are usually **polymaths** (skilled in many areas) and have broad rather than narrow interests. They are well-read and make connections between all disciplines, see relationships and analogies, and find inspiration in all fields, never limiting themselves to one area.
- Finally, geniuses are usually assumed to be novel, **out of the box thinkers**. Such people are non-conventional and tend to disregard arbitrary rules, fashions or unquestioned assumptions and habits. They are comfortable pushing outside of the norms and exploring new territory – and this makes them natural innovators and trendsetters. (as well as problem solvers!).
- We can always be aware of these mindsets and deliberately work to cultivate them in ourselves, in a variety of ways.

Chapter 2: Mozart and the Empty Pitcher

What better place to begin our discussion on the idea of genius than with the world's most well-known musical child prodigy, Mozart. While many of the geniuses in the rest of our book took time to make a name for themselves, Mozart was recognized as a genius pretty much from childhood.

His father was a music teacher, and his home was filled with instruments. When he was just four years old, Mozart asked to be taught to play piano, and soon his dedication and talent was evident. His other teachers also noticed not just his speed at acquiring new pieces, but the ease with which he embellished and expanded on them. It was plain to everyone around him: he was a born composer.

At six, Mozart was touring and performing in cities all over Europe, fully supporting the family financially. Yes, that's right – he was a celebrated, working musician just *two years* after learning to play the piano.

The obvious question is, *how?* We can look to many different factors:

- Mozart is said to have been partly driven by jealousy and the pressure to live up to his older sister, who was also an extremely talented pianist.
- He was placed under considerable pressure by his father, perhaps something of a thwarted genius himself, whom Mozart tried all his life to impress.
- He not only had an aptitude for music, but also a genuine interest in it.
- He grew up in a musical home and a cultural milieu that recognized and rewarded musical excellence.
- His innate musical talent was relentlessly cultivated from an extremely young age. Mozart was encouraged to perform and practice with no other obligations.

Looking at this list, you might get the impression that Mozart's life was extremely structured, ordered, and rigid. In fact, the opposite was true, and it may be very his lack of shape that constituted his unique genius. Mozart may have been an early practitioner of the "empty pitcher" approach.

Picture it this way: you have a giant water pitcher. You fill this pitcher up to the very brim, but then you keep going and fill it up even further. What happens? The water simply overflows. The pitcher can only hold so much. In fact, once it's full of water, that's it. The pitcher has served its function, and in a way, has become useless.

If we imagine that our mind is like this pitcher, and that water is like creative inspiration or new ideas, we can easily see the power of the analogy: when we are already filled with pre-existing ideas, there simply is no room for any more. We can keep the tap running, so to speak, but that incoming learning and insight will simply flow right past us.

This concept is similar to one found in Buddhist lore: the pitcher is only useful when it's empty. The paradox is that the emptiness inside the pitcher is actually its value. Similarly, our value lies in our *potential*, and our best work may emerge from stillness, emptiness, pauses, or learning to encounter the "white space" within us.

The creative process can't be held too tightly
Though Mozart likely knew nothing of far Eastern philosophy, he may have intuited this principle and lived out its lesson in his own life. He was well known for his constant pursuit of leisure activities, daydreaming, rambling, and wandering without aim... and of spontaneously coming up with new composition ideas

seemingly from thin air. He was, in other words, very good at being an empty pitcher!

Mozart's purported composition process was an exercise in free-form, emergent creation. He would lay blank music sheets onto a billiard table, roll a billiard ball so it bounced off two edges, then quickly scribble a note down on the paper, catching the ball before it could bounce a third time. He would repeat this and put down the next note, then the next, never giving his conscious mind too much time to mull over its work.

Now, of course this idiosyncratic method is not going to work for everything, but it does point to the kind of approach that young Mozart took to his own work. It shows how he appreciated the value of that "white space" and how, despite all the pressures and expectations around him, he knew that the well of creativity was best pursued obliquely, in a relaxed, receptive, and open-minded way. Mozart knew that sometimes our best work is done in the "empty" space between thoughts, and in the few split seconds between the bounces of a billiard ball. He did not sit down at a desk to grind away at his work like a machine. Instead, he was relaxed, playful, and even a little irreverent.

Use the "Mozart Method" in your own life
What follows is a technique inspired by and derived from many of Mozart's purported work methods, but of course, use discretion and

creativity in adjusting these steps to fit your own goals, talents, and limitations.

Step 1: Choose a "mindless" activity

In the billiards example described above, Mozart used a physical/mechanical activity to distract yet also focus him. The bounce of the ball takes as much time as it takes, and the act of following it with your eyes and catching it in time is just enough mental diversion to "get out of your head." Then, *without thinking at all*, you make a decision, and act. Without pausing to think about what you've just done, you keep going. The melody takes shape on the page, but you are not watching it too closely. You are getting out of your own way, and leaving absolutely no time in which your self-critical or second-guessing mind can chip in and derail you.

The first step is to decide which physical activity *you* can use to distract your own conscious mind in the same way. This depends to some degree on your task, but also on what is likely to count as a mindless activity for you personally. You could walk the dog, bounce a ball against the wall, take a shower, mow the lawn, cook soup, or do a simple yet repetitive task like knit, doodle, or clean. Whatever it is, the task should require zero thought yet keep you physically distracted.

Step 2: Let your mind go

Start your mindless activity, and then... keep going. Be very loose and undirected about it. You are not really "doing" anything, but rather just permitting your mind to go where it wants. Have no plan, and no expectations. Imagine just "letting it all hang out" - mentally, that is!

The idea is that your unconscious mind can go off and do whatever it likes while you are physically occupied with your task. You are not *trying* to do it, or to do anything at all to help the process along. Remember, all you are doing is knitting the next row or putting one foot in front of the other. Finding "white space" in this way is profoundly relaxing and yet strangely focusing and energizing at the same time. Practice often enough and the process may start to feel meditative.

Step 3: Have your capture device ready

Mozart ensured that he always had music paper and a pen ready at hand. This was his method of capturing whatever the process produced. Depending on your activity, your work, and your preferences, your capture device could be pen and paper, but it could also be craft materials, models, instruments, tools, a video or audio recorder, or even a person you can instantly share ideas with.

The point is that once you have emptied your mind and allowed it to spontaneously fill will fresh, new ideas, you need to make sure you are ready to catch them when they appear. Don't fall into the trap of thinking that you can always make some notes later – some of the world's best ideas have been lost this way! Instead, jot them down immediately. Then, forget about it and keep going. You can return to it all later and process it in a more proactive, conscious way.

When Mozart said, "the music is not in the notes, but in the silence between", the above process may just have been what he was alluding to.

Pour out. Fill up again. Repeat.
It would be a misunderstanding of the "Mozart Method" to assume that emptying the pitcher alone is all that's required. Mozart was able to spontaneously generate new ideas because:

a) He possessed a measure of innate talent.
b) He had an extensive musical training and background to draw on.

Mozart said, "People err who think my art comes easily to me. I assure you, dear friend, nobody has devoted so much time and thought to compositions as I. There is not a famous master whose music I have not industriously studied through many times." Yes, he was a child prodigy and a genius, and yes, he was prolific and successful. Yet he also worked *extraordinarily hard*. Considering that he was essentially working to support his family at the tender age of six, Mozart bore enormous responsibility and endured pressure that many adults might crumble under – not unlike some child stars today!

The point is that geniuses often know how to combine deep work with genuine rest and play. Structured, diligent practice is best interspersed with frequent opportunity to disengage, let loose, and empty the mind.

Have you ever come up with a surprisingly novel idea from out of the blue while showering? It is during periods of rest that the brain can recuperate enough to start spontaneously generating material of its own – rather than being asked to constantly respond to a stream of information coming its way.

This should put a new perspective on the modern habit of endless scrolling, gaming, or TV. While the brain is engaging in these activities, it is *not* daydreaming or resting, nor is it practicing, learning, or studying. This state of mind is arguably the worst of both worlds! For some people, their brains are "on" from the moment they wake up in the morning, so that the first time they ever get their thoughts to themselves is when they collapse into bed… and then they immediately start to ruminate and churn over all the things they haven't had any space to genuinely process during the day.

You don't have to practice the deliberate method outlined above to start deriving benefits from more rest and nondirected activity in your life. Try:

- Switching activities throughout the day. Mix up physical and mental tasks, change rooms, or take a new perspective on the same task.
- Take frequent breaks of different lengths – and not just to scroll online or zone out in front of the TV.
- Have a nap or just meditate quietly for a moment, doing nothing.
- Do some exercise, stretch, or just take some deep belly breaths to reconnect to your body and give your brain the chance to reset.
- Socializing can also help you switch gears and distract yourself, especially if you've been working on a hard-to-solve problem.
- Make room for unstructured and non-directed activity. Make space to doodle, make mistakes, mess around, and explore. Not everything has to be serious all the time.
- Don't let what you already know grow stale or stagnant. Occasionally throw everything out and start again.
- Play! Again, try to avoid screen time that only stresses or numbs you, and instead go for engrossing and nonaddictive activities, particularly those that promote mind-body connection.

Mozart worked hard, but he also knew how to cultivate creative emptiness. Returning to our pitcher metaphor: try to imagine that work, creativity, and innovation are a cycle of routinely emptying yourself and allowing yourself to be filled up again. You become like a useful pitcher in constant use. Relax, let your mind wander, and then come back to your task, ready to work hard again. Then repeat.

Summary:

- **Mozart's genius traits: ability to empty the mind and pursue inspiration and rest obliquely, interspersing this with deep work.**
- One of Mozart's methods for composing included quick, spontaneous action that allowed his conscious mind to take a back seat.
- Practice this method yourself by choosing a mindless activity to engage in, let your mind go and make sure that you have a method of capture for all the insight and fresh ideas that flow into your newly empty "pitcher".
- To be more like Mozart: Build more creativity and find fresh inspiration. Give yourself permission to doodle, wander, mess around, experiment, ramble, or simply do something unconnected to your field of study. This will allow your conscious mind to rest and recharge, while your unconscious mind can generate something new to fill the "white space."

Chapter 3: Einstein and Combinatorial Play

Albert Einstein is the world-renowned German physicist and mathematician who won the Nobel Prize in 1921 for his work on the photoelectric effect. Now considered one of the most influential scientific theorists in history, Einstein was known for being a deeply inquisitive and curious person. Reportedly Einstein didn't enjoy school as a child, but early tutoring experiences sparked his interest in the topic of light.

Excusing himself from military service as a young man and dropping out of school (he preferred independent study), his parents were worried about his future. Nevertheless, he was admitted to a prestigious Zurich university because of his excellent performance on the math and physics entrance exams. After graduating he worked as a patent clerk, where he privately pursued some of his own ideas.

In 1905 he published four breakthrough papers on the photoelectric effect, Brownian motion and relativity. Einstein married and had children, but his marriage was not a happy one, and he divorced and remarried in 1919. At the time, Einstein was less known for his theory of relativity than he is today, and perhaps could not have predicted the full direction his discoveries would take physics in the future (for example, his work foreshadowing the development of the atomic bomb).

Einstein: not a one-trick pony

Surprisingly (or perhaps not), the most notable scientist of the 20th century was also known for taking time out of his research to play the violin. In so doing, Einstein was engaging in a combination of the "hard" and the "soft" or, more accurately, he was exercising skills that required very different mindsets.

Reportedly, he was even very good at the instrument, as he was with the piano. But while sawing away on the violin during his breaks, Einstein actually arrived at some breakthroughs in his research and philosophical questionings. Allegedly one of these musical sessions was the spark for his most famous equation: $E=mc^2$. Knowing what we know about how true genius sees the world, this shouldn't surprise us.

Einstein came up with the term *combinatory play* to describe the intangible process in which his favorite pastime led to ideas that revolutionized the whole of scientific thought. He explained his reasoning as best he could in 1945 in a letter to French mathematician Jacques S. Hadamard:

> *"My Dear Colleague:*
>
> *In the following, I am trying to answer in brief your questions as well as I am able. I am not satisfied myself with those answers and I am willing to answer more questions if you believe this could be of any advantage for the very interesting and difficult work you have undertaken.*
>
> *(A) The words or the language, as they are written or spoken, do not seem to play any role in my mechanism of thought. The psychical entities which seem to serve as elements in thought are certain signs and more or less clear images which can be "voluntarily" reproduced and combined.*
>
> *There is, of course, a certain connection between those elements and relevant logical concepts. It is also clear that the desire to arrive finally at logically connected concepts is the emotional basis of this rather vague play with the above-mentioned elements. But taken from a psychological viewpoint, this combinatory play seems to be the essential feature in*

productive thought—before there is any connection with logical construction in words or other kinds of signs which can be communicated to others.

(B) The above-mentioned elements are, in my case, of visual and some of muscular type. Conventional words or other signs have to be sought for laboriously only in a secondary stage, when the mentioned associative play is sufficiently established and can be reproduced at will.

(C) According to what has been said, the play with the mentioned elements is aimed to be analogous to certain logical connections one is searching for.

(D) Visual and motor. In a stage when words intervene at all, they are, in my case, purely auditive, but they interfere only in a secondary stage, as already mentioned.

(E) It seems to me that what you call full consciousness is a limit case which can never be fully accomplished. This seems to be connected with the fact called the narrowness of consciousness (Enge des Bewusstseins)."

Notice, firstly, that Einstein has no problem with metacognition, or thinking about his own thinking and asking questions about his own question-asking. Einstein seemed to believe that indulging in his creative tendencies was helpful for his logical and rational pursuits. That might have been the case, and it also might have been the case that to engage in a distraction was helpful for taking on different perspectives and viewing problems from different angles. Perhaps it's related to the so-called Medici effect, in which the melding of different disciplines will inevitably lead to new discoveries, and the whole always seems to be greater than the sum of the parts.

Indeed, combinatory play is not simply the notion that *play* takes your mind to a different world to regroup. It recognizes, as Einstein did, that taking pieces of knowledge and insight from different disciplines and combining them in new contexts is how most creativity truly happens. So as mentioned, somehow Einstein saw something in playing the violin that helped him think about physics in an entirely new way.

The lesson here is to engage in your own pursuits and not feel constrained by having to stay in similar or adjacent disciplines, thinking that only they will aid you. There are *always* parallels between different disciplines, so find them. More of the same probably will not help; a dash of something different just might.

The power of the possible
Einstein became well-known for another thinking technique, and it is one that we use most days in everyday life.

"What if humans were capable of flying?"

"What if the world's landmasses never broke up into separate continents and instead remained as Pangaea to this day?"

These are hypothetical "what if" questions that tickle your mind into thinking from other perspectives and challenge you to question your premises. Imagining hypotheticals goes beyond simple thinking skills that require only memorization, description of an observable event or situation, or even analysis of facts and concrete events. Because hypotheticals pose questions about what isn't, what hasn't happened, or what isn't likely to ever happen, they stretch the imagination in new ways and sharpen creative thinking and practical intelligence. They allow a person to try on different perspectives as though they were lenses, and suddenly see what was invisible to them before.

For instance, you've never considered the implications of human flight because it's impossible, so there is a world of thoughts that have remained unexplored. How would traffic lights work, what kind of licensing process would be required, would we still have cars and airplanes, and how would safety work? Now, how would those rules and laws apply to normal traffic situations in the present day? Think through the realities of how everything would fit together—it's no small feat!

Hypothetical situations taken to the extreme are thought experiments, and Albert Einstein in particular was known to use these. He called them *Gedankenexperiments*, which is German for "thought experiments."

A thought experiment, in a more general context, is essentially playing out a "what if" scenario to its end. It's acting as if a theory or hypothesis were true, diving deep into the ramifications and seeing what happens to your "what if" under intense scrutiny. A thought experiment allows you to analyze interesting premises you could never manifest in reality and make new leaps of logic and discovery because you can consider conditions that current knowledge doesn't yet reach.

Suppose the problem situation is needing to exit a room. The conventional ways to do so are to walk out the door or jump out the window. But what if the door is blocked by a raging fire and the room is on the tenth floor of the building? These conditions have now rendered your conventional solutions fatal. You can only get out of the room either by finding a way to kill that fire or by having the capacity to survive a fall of several hundred feet. Something in this scenario needs to drastically change its usage or definition, or it will break entirely. This is the essence of the thought experiment. *Suppose this happens. What happens next? And then? And then?*

Thought experiments were one of Einstein's superpowers. He could imagine a scenario, play it out mentally with shocking accuracy and detail, and then extract the subtle conclusions that lay within.

One of Einstein's most famous *Gedankenexperiments* begins with a simple premise: what would happen if you chased and then eventually caught up to and rode a beam of light through space? In theory, once you caught up to the beam of light, it would appear to be frozen next to you because you are moving at the same speed. Just like if you are walking at the same pace as a car driving next to you, there is no acceleration (the relative velocities are the same), so the car would seem to be stuck to your side.

The only problem was that this was an impossible proposition at the turn of the century. If you catch up to the light and the light appears to be frozen right next to you, then it is inherently impossible that it is light, because of the difference in speeds. It ceases to be light at that moment. This means one of the rules of physics was broken or disproved with this elementary thought.

Therefore, one of the assumptions that underlay physics at the time had to change, and Einstein realized that the assumption of time as a constant had to shift. This discovery directly laid the path for the theory of relativity. The closer you get to the speed the light, the more time becomes different for you—relative to an outside observer.

This thought experiment allowed Einstein to challenge what were thought to be set-in-stone rules set forth by Isaac Newton's three laws of energy and matter. This thought experiment was instrumental in realizing that people should have questioned old models and fundamental "rules" instead of trying to conform their theories to them.

Einstein's strengths
Let's return now to the genius traits we mentioned in the previous chapter, and see how Einstein measures against them. As we saw

above, we can see that many of Einstein's great *Eureka* moments came from his being a **polymath**, or "cross-pollinating" ideas from one area to another (in this case music and physics). It's probably quite obvious that another of Einstein's strengths was **intellectual curiosity**, lust for learning and insatiable desire to keep asking questions. We can see so much of the lighthearted, uninhibited child aspect of genius in Einstein, who literally labelled a technique he used as "play."

Einstein never set out to win any prizes, or earn accolades as the best physicist of his generation. That was never his goal. Rather, he simply wanted to *understand*. His passion for seeing into the deeper nature of things led him to areas of knowledge that were previously uncharted. We can see how this attitude put him at odds with his more conventional, pedagogical early school life, and we can imagine that the young Einstein would not have been much inspired by boring lessons about things that were already well known and established.

We cannot imagine Einstein's great achievements happening without his enormous sense of curiosity spurring him on. He was not motivated by pride or fame, either, since he was known to regularly alienate and offend other scientists and peers and was reportedly quite difficult to work with. Einstein was nothing if not a curious soul, and it's this attitude of inquiry that seems to have informed his entire life.

We can see in Einstein's case that curiosity so often comes with **non-conventionality**. He was a "draft dodger" and concocted a medical excuse so as not to complete military service, and was not averse to skipping classes or generally failing to follow school rules. He seemed to have little regard for pre-established hierarchies and preferred to trust his own estimations of what was important and worth doing. And, this trait, too, is at the center of his success. Can you imagine any scientist being credited with completely paradigm-shifting work in the field *without* completely breaking the rules of the day?

We know and love Einstein today as a fiercely smart, independent thinker who greatly advanced the human scientific endeavor. But we need to remember that Einstein was just a man, who at one time saw his own vision only dimly, and worked on his pursuits with no guarantee of where they would lead. The one thing that can motivate a person through such a path? Endless curiosity. We can imagine that Einstein would have been fulfilled even if he had never won any awards and died completely unknown.

Summary:

- **Einstein's Genius traits: Curiosity, broad area of interest (being a polymath), non-conventionality.**

- Einstein is known today as one of the 20th Century's most influential scientific thinkers, and was considered by many to be a genius in both mathematics and physics. He won the Nobel Prize for his work on the photoelectric effect, but he is best known today for his groundbreaking theory of relativity and his famous $e=mc^2$ equation.

- Einstein coined his own term for the kind of playful, free form connections he'd make between different topics and ideas: combinatorial play. By putting two unrelated ideas together to create something new, Einstein often solved problems, came up with creative new ideas or opened new avenues of thoughts to pursue.

- The game of "what if?" is another way to flex the curiosity muscle and bring freshness and novelty to conventional thinking. By running hypothetical situations and thought experiments in his mind, Einstein satisfied his thirst for learning and understanding, and accessed new insights that were beyond conventions at the time.

- Einstein was a polymath, and had a broad range of interests, rather than just one narrow focus. He played violin and piano, and had some of his best new ideas during play. This kind of broad mindedness and diversity of interest promotes intellectual agility and wide-ranging, flexible perspectives.

- Einstein was also non-conventional and worked independently, regardless of the established rules that surrounded him in early life. This allowed him to engage in truly independent ideas and contribute something entirely different to the field.

- We can see in Einstein's case that non-linearity of thought, insatiable curiosity and a wide range of interests were not just helpful to his success, but essential. We can follow suit by freely engaging in combinatorial play and "what if?" games in the areas that grab our intense interest.

- Though conventions may occasionally be useful, the best territory to explore is that which is uncharted!

- **To be more like Einstein, we can think of ways to break down artificial limits and categories in our own thinking, and blend concepts and ideas together freely – can you think of a way to combine two of your interests to produce a third, completely new idea?**

Chapter 4: Be Prolifically Productive like Picasso

What comes to mind when you think about famous 20th Century painter Pablo Picasso?

Perhaps you instantly imagine the characteristic deconstructed faces in bright colors? The simple structured shapes, the cubism, or the figures that somehow appear to emerge from chaotically assembled pieces?

Appreciating Picasso's contribution to the art world would require a whole book and not just a chapter. With his characteristic use of line, perspective, and collage, Picasso demonstrated not only his aesthetic innovation, but his ability to truly think outside the box. Today we are familiar with his method of deconstruction and the emotional messages conveyed by his work, so it's difficult to appreciate just how groundbreaking his aesthetic really was at the time.

What concerns us, however, is another, perhaps less appreciated aspect of his genius: the fact that the man was an art-making *machine*. Picasso was almost the definition of "prolific." He produced around 147,800 works during his 78-year long career, which included 13,500 paintings, 100,000 engravings and prints, 34,000 sketches and illustrations, and 300 sculptures. Just take a moment to consider the energy and time required to produce *hundreds of thousands* of separate works of art!

Yes, Picasso was talented and innovative, but above all he was active, beginning to make art at just 7 years of age and continuing until his death. Young Picasso began sketching the moment he could hold a pencil, and as soon as he had mastered the basics of the academic art instruction he received, he began to rebel against the rules and create his own way.

Picasso was forcefully unconventional, insistent, and precocious, achieving at levels far beyond his peers. But this was no idle thing – he was known for working 14-hour days, and working late into the night, frequently painting from 5pm the evening before to 4am the following morning. He would then take a quick break before starting again at 6am and going until sunset, pausing only for an hour's lunch.

Frankly, his work ethic bordered on the obsessive.

Now, does this mean that if you want to think like a genius you need to forego sleep and regular meals? Of course not! But we do need a realistic understanding of the sacrifice, dedication, and sheer hard work required. Genius, then, is not something we are, but rather something we do. Picasso gave his life to artistic expression, and almost every waking moment was laid at that altar. But this sacrifice was not abstract or merely intellectual. "Action is the foundational key to all success" he once said, and his life of consistent effort proves that he took his own advice.

Reconsider your attitude to "work"
Earlier, we made the claim that Picasso often "worked" for 14-hour days... but did he? Picasso is recorded as thinking of painting as akin to "keeping a diary." It was something he couldn't help but do in order to document his life. For Picasso, painting was a way to think, to feel, and to engage with life. It was simply his way of *being*. This is a very different attitude to the one evoked by the word "work."

We all know that consistent effort and focused practice day in and day out are the only real ways to achieve growth and success. But our attitudes to this fact can vary, and some ways of thinking about "work" can drastically increase our productivity compared to others.

Picasso painted, sculpted, sketched, and scribbled relentlessly, almost with the same ease as he might breathe or move. To achieve something near his level of output, we need to start thinking of our own intellectual and creative efforts in the same way. Taking action, then, should not be perceived as some rare and exceptional event, or something we need to work up to or talk ourselves into. Rather, it should be the default – something that happens automatically and which would take more effort to *not* do than to do.

For this we need daily habits, routines, and systems that run all on their own. We need consistent action that builds and maintains momentum. Picasso produced nearly 300,000 pieces in his time, which seems like an unthinkably large number. It works out to 3800 works a year, and 315 works per month, which still sounds intimidating. But, if you "work" for 14 hours a day, that leaves you with more than an hour to create each piece. That "piece" here may include something as simple as a line drawing or a scribble. It doesn't seem quite so impossible now, right?

We can learn a few very important things about productivity from Picasso:

- "Take care of the quantity, and the quality will take care of itself."

- Commit and be dedicated – regardless of your chosen field of mastery, you will not get there by being part-time or lukewarm.
- Make strategic action a habit, rather than an occasional exception.
- Always be acting. Action is what keeps you moving, evolving, growing, and learning.

Thinking, brainstorming, planning, and contemplating are certainly useful activities. Yet they mean little until there is something to anchor them into the real world and bring them into being – the only thing that can do that is action. Picasso didn't think for hours about what he would paint or sketch. His painting and sketching *was* his thinking. He experimented, asked questions, and made plans, but he did all of this through his constant action and creation. How might you do the same for your own chosen area of mastery?

Embrace exponential action
So, Picasso saw making art as a way of thinking, feeling, being, documenting, and expressing his life. It was an extension of who he was. Very broadly, he spent his life averaging around one "artistic output" per hour. But a big part of Picasso's drive was not to simply rack up the numbers or churn out pieces like he was a factory. That was not at all his vision of "productivity."

Instead, Picasso's near continuous stream of output can be better understood as *one single, lifelong work* – a great conversation with life that played out over many separate episodes, expressions, and scenes. These works were connected to one another. They expressed the artist's ongoing and evolving transformation – which is why art historians so frequently refer to his work as progressive. These are not many isolated depictions, but a single story.

Considered this way, we can see each of Picasso's works as a re-iteration of all the previous ones. They are proof of development and maturation - of both the themes being explored, and the artist himself.

Picasso believed in setting clear goals, and the drive to reach that point created a line of consistency from every first attempt right to its fulfilment. In a sense, Picasso was no different from the inventors and innovators discussed elsewhere in this book; they all were feverishly seeking that desired endpoint, with each attempt bringing them closer. Seen in this light, prolific productivity is not the outcome at all, but rather the side effect of yearning for the ideal. How many of Picasso's tens of thousands of works can we consider a byproduct or even a waste material of the bigger artistic process?

"Our goals can only be reached through a vehicle of a plan, in which we must fervently believe, and upon which we must vigorously act." Picasso's art is the paper left by this "vehicle" and the vigorous action it left in its wake.

If you wish to capture some of this sentiment in your own life, it's crucial to keep checking in with your own true north, i.e. that magnetic endpoint that is igniting your yearning and calling you irresistibly to it. Once you know what really drives you, then productivity itself is no longer a goal nor a burden, but simply a means to your end.

Knowing your higher purpose and the goal that fires you up will allow you to embark on each new day with direction and energy. Every active step you take brings you a little bit closer.

Create a conducive environment

Picasso thrived on routine, but that required a dedicated workspace.

While his work might have been incredibly driven, focused, and obsessive, that doesn't mean any of it could have happened by accident. Creating art requires easy access to the right materials, light, space, and opportunity. The irony is that artists need to be relaxed and receptive to creative inspiration, but when it strikes, they had better be sure they have all the *practical* details in place!

Picasso actually had a name for his studio – La Boetie – and he considered it a sanctuary where both he and fellow artist Georges Braque could create some of their most recognizable works.

The environment you surround yourself with can be thought of as an extension of your own mind and creative will. It is a meta-tool - the place where you forge new ideas, experiment, and do everything necessary to bring your vision into concrete reality.

To that end, an environment that encourages genius is anything that inspires strategic action, and actively works to keep distraction and stress at bay. As an artist, Picasso's environment contained tools and spaces that stimulated and supported creativity – almost as though the room itself were a blank slate. But the environment best conducive to *your* genius will probably look very different.

Set up an environment for yourself that makes consistent, exponential action the most likely thing to occur. Picasso described how wine and music in his environment were conducive to art, but your magic ingredients may be silence, warmth, beautiful pictures, inspiring vision boards, plenty of strong coffee, challenging books, perfectly organized and color-coded stationery, a seat you can sit in for hours, high quality pens, or just a snack you like and a pair of slippers.

The right environment is like the oyster that can make a beautiful pearl over time. The only thing remaining is to implement daily, weekly, and monthly schedules that keep you in that productive environment as often as possible, for as long as possible. A few things to consider:

You don't have to wake up super early or work late into the night; be a true nonconformist and work when it best suits *you*. Your first act of creativity may be to design a workflow and schedule that truly fits you and your shifting energy levels.

Learn to say no. Picasso was not known for being a good cook, or for mastering Chinese poetry, or for having a well-organized shed. He chose *one thing*, and focused on that to the exclusion of all others. In the same way, learn to (politely) say no to everything that is not somehow connected to your ultimate vision.

Finally, keep adjusting. Your thoughts, daily routine, and mindset will change and shift as you go along – no human pursuit would be worth much if it didn't transform you in these ways, right? That means you need to periodically reappraise your process. What's working, and what isn't?

Summary :

- **Picasso's genius traits: ultra-productivity, the ability to constantly**

prioritize action, deep focus, and the maintenance of supportive environments.

- Picasso was almost unbelievably prolific, and spent nearly all of his time on his craft. His attitude was not that he was "working", but rather living his obsession, which is more like a life-long passion than an obligation.

- Picasso was always experimenting iteratively, and made constant progressive movement towards his ideal vision using exponential action.

- Picasso set aside a dedicated creative sanctuary reserved only for painting.

- **To be more like Picasso, commit fully to your vision. Set clear boundaries and priorities, and say no to distractions and anything not related to your goal. Make strategic action a habit, rather than an occasional exception, and never stop experimenting.**

Chapter 5: Socrates' Endless Questions

One of the purest and most obvious ways to engage and practice our curiosity is to ask questions. Nothing could more plainly reflect a hunger for understanding, the student's mindset, or a willingness to open up to the new and unknown. The scientific method can be thought of as a kind of formalized way to ask questions of the universe, and a way to shape our inquiry and interpret the answers we get. But it all starts with questions (even questions like, "what if...?").

When it comes to the art of asking questions, we need look no further than Socrates, whose style of questioning his own thinking, the thinking of others and reality itself has come to be called the Socratic method.

Good questions end up allowing us to *triangulate* understanding. Take a textbook, for example. It is necessarily broad and cannot hope to cover all the subtleties involved. If we fully accept what we read, then we are set on a singular path. If we ask questions, we are able to see that the path itself contains twists and turns and may not even be accurate. Different lines of inquiry are generated, and it is understood that there are multiple paths, each with their own perspective. Questions allow us to both clarify misunderstandings and reinforce what we already know. In the end, we come to an understanding of the same textbook that is nuanced and more accurate.

Luckily for us, teachers have known this for literally thousands of years. The most helpful framework for generating insightful questions comes from none other than Socrates himself, the ancient Greek philosopher perhaps best known for being Plato's teacher, as well as being executed by the state for "corrupting the minds of the youth." His method of teaching was largely in the form of dialogues and questions, appropriately called the *Socratic Method*.

Socrates himself wrote nothing during his lifetime, but we can see his philosophy expounded in the works of Plato and other contemporaries. In these plays and dialogues, Socrates was described as someone who was deeply insightful, curious, and in possession of incredible mastery over language and logical argument. Nevertheless, he was a controversial figure in his time, and offended many, since his criticism of much of Athenian culture and politics at the time were considered impious.

During his life, Socrates and his work were often mocked and derided in plays and writings, and it was mainly after his death that his followers attempted to preserve his contributions in the form of written dialogues, essentially conversations between him and themselves.

Unfortunately, because Socrates lived so long ago, historians have little information on who he was as a person, beyond the ideas communicated by his contemporaries and followers. Nevertheless, even with the fragments we do have, and by reading his works, we can recognize something of the genius traits that have not changed much in the thousands of years since Socrates lived. When it comes to curiosity, intellectual honesty and patience, we may be hard pressed to find an individual who better demonstrates these traits than Socrates.

Understanding the spirit of the Socratic Method

When you boil it down, the Socratic Method is when you ask questions upon questions in an effort to dissect an assertion or statement for greater understanding. The person asking the questions might seem like they are on the offensive, but they are asking questions to enrich both parties and discover the underlying assumptions and motivations of the assertion or statement. It is from this process that we have a framework for effective questioning.

Imagine that you make a proclamation, and the only response you get is a smug, "Oh, is that so? What about X and Y?" Unfortunately, the know-it-all questioner is on the right path.

American law schools are notorious for using the Socratic Method. A professor will ask a student a question, and then the student will have to defend their statement against a professor's questioning regarding the merits of a case or law. It's not adversarial by nature, but it does force someone to explain their reasoning and logic—and of course, gaps in knowledge and logical flaws will probably surface. This process serves the goal of deeper understanding and insight. It may cause defensiveness, though it is not offensive in itself.

So what exactly is the Socratic Method, beyond asking a series of tough questions that make people uncomfortable? When you do it to yourself, you are forcing understanding. You are putting yourself through an incredible stress test that will make you question yourself and your logic. It will force you to discard your assumptions and see what you might be missing. If you are mercilessly questioned and picked apart with Socratic questioning, what remains afterward will be deeply comprehended and validated. If there is an error in your thinking or a gap in your understanding, it will be found, corrected, and proofed with a rebuttal. That's deep learning.

Applied curiosity

As a brief example, imagine you are telling someone that the sky is blue.

This seems like an unquestionable statement that is an easy truth. Obviously, the sky is blue. You've known that since you were a child. You go outside and witness it each day. You've told someone that their eyes were as blue as the sky. But remember, our goal with questions is to better acquire knowledge as to the sky's blueness. So imagine someone asks *why* you know it is blue.

There are many ways to answer that question, but you decide to say that you know the sky is blue because it reflects the ocean, and that the ocean is blue, even though this is erroneous. The questioner asks how you know it is a reflection of the ocean.

How would you answer this?

This brief line of Socratic questioning just revealed that you have no idea why or how the sky reflects (or doesn't) the blue of the planet's oceans. You just attempted to explain an underlying assumption, and you were mildly surprised to discover that you had no idea.

This is the profound starting point of the Socratic method – we are assumed to know nothing, and nothing is taken as a given. We make our minds blank and attempt to simply observe, to reason, from scratch, and to see where we arrive, without falling back on guesses, assumptions, denials or outright lies. In a way, this open-mindedness is the heart of real curiosity. Have you ever noticed how a small child keeps asking "why?" after everything you say? They are not operating from the same foregone conclusions that you as an adult are, and they genuinely don't know. Everything is new to them. Though slightly annoying, this frame of mind is the one most likely to perceive genuinely, to understand, and to be most receptive to new discovery. Geniuses are not those that have all the answers, it turns out, but rather all the questions!

Curiosity, in a nutshell, is the heart of the Socratic Method. A series of innocent and simple questions directed at yourself, honestly and earnestly answered, can unravel what you thought you knew and lead you to understand exactly what you don't know. This is often just as important as knowing what you *do* know because it uncovers your blind spots and weaknesses. Recall that the method was used by teachers as a teaching tool, so it is designed to impart deeper understanding and clarify ambiguities.

There are six types of Socratic questions as delineated by R.W. Paul. After just briefly glancing at this list, you might understand how these questions can improve your learning and lead you to fill in the gaps in your knowledge.

The six types of questions are:

1. Clarification questions—why exactly does it matter?
2. Probing assumptions—what hidden assumptions might exist?
3. Probing rationale, reasons, evidence—what proven evidence exists?
4. Questioning viewpoints and perspectives—what other perspectives exist?
5. Probing implications and consequences—what does this mean, what is the significance, and how does it connect to other information?
6. Questions about the question—why is this question important?

Clarification questions: What is the real meaning of what is being said? Is there an underlying hidden motivation or significance to this piece of information? What do they hope to achieve with it? Suppose we have the same assertion from above, where the sky is blue. Here are some sample questions from each category you could plausibly ask to gain clarity and challenge their thoughts.

- What does it matter to you if the sky is blue?
- What is the significance to you?
- What is the main issue here?
- What exactly do you mean by that?
- What does that have to do with the rest of the discussion?
- Why would you say that?

Probing assumptions: What assumptions are the assertions based on, and are they actually supported by evidence? What is opinion and belief, and what is evidence-based fact or proven in some other way? Unless you are reading a scientific paper, there are always inherent assumptions that may or may not be accurate.

- Is your blue my blue?
- Why do you think the sky is blue?
- How can you prove or verify that?
- Where is this coming from exactly?
- So what leads you to believe the sky is blue?
- How can you prove that the sky is blue?

Probing rationale, reasons, and evidence: How do you know the evidence is trustworthy and valid? What are the conclusions drawn, and what rationale, reasons, and evidence are specifically used in such a way? What might be missing or glazed over?

- What's the evidence for the sky's color, and why is it convincing?
- How exactly does the ocean's reflection color the sky?
- What is an example of that?
- Why do you think that is true?
- What if the information was incorrect or flawed?
- Can you tell me the reasoning?

Questioning viewpoints and perspectives: People will almost always present an assertion or argument from a specific bias, so play the devil's advocate and remain skeptical about what they have come up with. Ask why opposing viewpoints and perspectives aren't preferred and why they don't work.

- How else could your evidence be interpreted, an alternative view?
- Why is that research the best in proving that the sky is blue?
- Could the same be said about proving the sky is red? Why or why not?
- What are the potential flaws in this argument?
- What is the counterargument?

- Why doesn't the sky color the ocean instead of the other way around?

Probing implications and consequences: What are the conclusions and why? What else could it mean, and why was this particular conclusion drawn? What will happen as a consequence, and why?

- If the sky is blue, what does that mean about reflections?
- Who is affected by the sky's color?
- What does this information mean, and what are the consequences?
- What does this finding imply? What else does it determine?
- How does it connect to the broader topic or narrative?
- If the sky is blue, what does that mean about the ocean?
- What else could your evidence and research prove about the planet?

Questions about the question: This is less effective when you are directing this question to yourself. Directed toward someone else, you are forcing people to ponder why you asked the question or why you went down that line of questioning, and realize that you had something you wanted to evoke. What did you mean when you said that, and why did you ask about X rather than Y?

- So why do you think I asked you about your belief in the sky's color?
- What do you think I wanted to do when I asked you about this?
- How do you think this knowledge might help you in other topics?
- How does this apply to everyday life and what we were discussing earlier?

At first, it sounds like a broken record, but there is a method to the madness. Each question may seem similar, but if answered correctly and adequately, they go in different directions. In the example of the blue sky, there are over twenty separate questions—twenty separate answers and probes into someone's simple assertion that the sky is blue. You can almost imagine how someone might discover that they know next to nothing and are only able to regurgitate a limited set of facts without context or understanding.

The Socratic Method is a thinking technique

You can apply the Socratic Method to ensure that you are understanding what you think you are. You can think of it as a systematic process of examining and just double-checking yourself. The end result will always be a win, as you either confirm your mastery or figure out exactly what is missing.

Suppose you hear from a friend that the Spanish Inquisition was a fairly humane process of light interrogation, with only minor maimings and lashings (various sources put the death toll at, on average, around one hundred thousand people). In this instance, you can use the Socratic questions to correct a mistake. The six question types, as a reminder:

1. Clarification questions—why does it matter?
2. Probing assumptions—what hidden assumptions might exist?
3. Probing rationale, reasons, evidence—what proven evidence exists?
4. Questioning viewpoints and perspectives—what other perspectives exist?
5. Probing implications and consequences—what does this mean, what is the significance, and how does it connect to other information?
6. Questions about the question—why is this question important?

To check the veracity of this statement, you might ask:

- What exactly is being said, and why does it matter?
- What is that statement based on?

- What makes you think it is true? Where's the evidence for it?
- Who might have this perspective, and why? What might be the opposing perspective? Why is that?
- What does this mean for Spanish history as a whole? Are all history textbooks incorrect? What else will be affected by this knowledge?
- Why do you think I might be asking you about this?

What about using the Socratic questions for deeper understanding of a topic, such as the biology of the brain? Actually, the questions don't change—all six of the above questions can be used in the same way to more deeply understand brain structures. You'll learn, you'll poke holes, and you'll understand. Isn't that what this whole thing is all about?

Turning the questions on ourselves

The Socratic method teaches us the power of asking questions, and how genuinely curious and open-minded inquiry is at the root of every new piece of understanding or learning. But to do this sort of thing well takes a lot more practice than it might first seem. In a way, it can sometimes be harder to get rid of our false assumptions and limiting beliefs than it is to comprehend something new and true from scratch.

Each of us has long held our own personal set of biases and prejudices, assumptions and personal worldviews that may or may not be accurate or helpful to us. When we ask honest and direct questions (even and especially of those things we completely take for granted) we can start to unpick those fixed and inaccurate mental habits. Nevertheless, we won't get far if we insist on lying to ourselves, denying facts, or clinging to certain ideas to protect our egos.

The Socratic method, in other words, is best practiced with healthy doses of intellectual honesty. One of the traits that was perhaps less pronounced in Einstein, in our previous chapter, is certainly evident here in Socrates' work. Having humility and being able to abandon an idea or belief in the face of evidence is not just a question of logic and awareness – it takes maturity to admit that you are wrong, or that you don't know something. It takes a certain kind of self-honesty to look at your way of thinking and admit that it could be better, or that certain presumptions have maybe been a little lazy or confused.

In Socrates' dialogues, both parties are not just having an ordinary conversation; the implication is that both are doing something noble – seeking the truth, with one another's aid. It is not a question of catching out the other, boasting or winning an argument – this is limited, ego-based thinking that will only trip up genuine understanding. Rather, Socrates uses his classic "gotcha!" moments to demonstrate, in real time, the irrationality of a certain position.

Socrates was famous for leading people down certain paths – he'd get them to agree to a series of statements and then present them with a conclusion that would immediately illustrate to them the error of their assumption. Or, he would "play dumb" and behave as if he knew nothing at all about a topic, so that he could, with the help of his conversation partner, piece together the ideas one step at a time. This the approach that most quickly reveals any hidden biases or incorrect assumptions.

Summary:

- **Socrates' Genius traits: Curiosity, intellectual honesty, non-conventionality.**

- Though not much is known about Socrates' personal life, his students and followers wrote down dialogues and plays containing some of his main ideas, where he demonstrated a heightened ability for rational argument and insight.
- Like other people considered great philosophical minds, Socrates took total ignorance as a starting point and cleared his mind so that he could inquire genuinely into the nature of things. His Socratic method is a

classic question-driven approach to seeking out knowledge and understanding.
- To practice this in our own lives, we can use 6 main types of questions to get to heart of a matter.
- We can ask clarification questions, questions that probe assumptions, probe rationale, reasons, and evidence, question viewpoints and perspectives, probe implications and consequences, and ask questions about the nature of the question itself.
- Our goal is to find out why certain ideas matter, to see what hidden or unconscious assumptions we hold, to look more rationally and closely at evidence, to consider and weigh up potential perspectives we haven't considered, to think about the meaning of the answer we are looking for and how it relates to other pieces of information we have, and to think about the way we are framing our question and why.
- The Socratic method can be used to inquire more deeply into our own beliefs, but it can also help us debate more effectively with others. We can use the fundamentals of Socratic dialogue to structure more logical arguments or design experiments that follow the scientific method, i.e. making a hypothesis (a question) and testing it against evidence and observation to reach an insightful conclusion.

- To be more like Socrates, we can get into the habit of routinely asking questions of our own deeply held beliefs and assumptions, taking nothing for granted. Be like the child who always asks, "but why?"

Chapter 6: Sun Tzu and Thinking Like a Warrior

While Picasso was a master at "the war of art," we now turn our attention to the master of "the art of war." Sun Tzu, the legendary Chinese general and philosopher who penned the book of the same name, has plenty to teach us about the genius inherent in the warrior's way of thinking.

It would be a mistake to think that genius is solely the domain of artists and scientists. The insight in *The Art of War* is that the battle metaphor really applies to everything in life. All physical conflicts, Sun Tzu taught, are also mental ones, because they begin and end in the mind. Thus, if we master "mental combat" we have won the more challenging, inner war – we have mastered ourselves.

On the surface, Sun Tzu's advice is about tactics, diplomacy, and military strategy; but it is also about learning to use the mind as a weapon. Strategy, in fact, allows us to subdue the enemy in unexpected ways, conserve resources, and employ wisdom and restraint instead of blunt force. To best our adversities, we improve ourselves first, ultimately learning to think more intelligently and quickly.

Though Sun Tzu's words are now almost 3000 years old, they easily resonate with us today when we understand his descriptions as allegories. He explains how to make decisions, strategize, plan, avoid loss, optimize, and pre-empt. He also explains that one must always be a step or two ahead of one's adversary.

True to the spirit of his ancient Confucian worldview, Sun Tzu's teaching is not about *what*, but more about *how*. Rather than list off a series of desirable actions, his is a game played with a particular attitude and mindset. We can turn to his military genius as a source of genius in overall "big picture" thinking and masterful decision-making – something that brilliant scientists and inventors are sometimes known to lack!

Now, while you're obviously not going to want to know how to battle and disarm smaller nations (right?), Sun Tzu can teach you about the psychology of battle and the supremacy of *strategy* in resolving all of life's problems. He can teach you tactics for defusing tension and neutralizing one's enemies. This comes close to helping us cultivate the *genius of living a truly good and successful life*, rather than merely achieving dominance in one or two isolated areas. Sun Tzu points us beyond mere personal productivity or understanding our own psychology, to the value of learning to understand others and the situations around us.

"If you know the enemy and know yourself, you need not fear the result of a hundred battles. If you know yourself but not the enemy, for every victory gained you will also suffer a defeat. If you know neither the enemy nor yourself, you will succumb in every battle."

The *Art of War* is broken into 13 concise chapters containing wide-ranging advice, and it's well worth a read. His aphorisms and advice include:

- Always opt for strategy over force – always know how and *whether* to fight.
- Knowledge is power. Honestly appraise facts without rash emotions distorting the picture.
- Little wins matter – conserve energy and opt to go with what's already working rather than losing momentum by changing tack too often.
- Be prepared and be patient. Ponder and deliberate. Always think of how things might unfold over time, rather than having tunnel vision and focusing on the present alone.

- Timing is everything. It is better to make small, effective moves precisely when they are needed, than thrash around and hope something sticks.
- Don't get cocky or rest on your laurels: "Do not repeat the tactics which have gained you one victory, but let your methods be regulated by the infinite variety of circumstances."

Below we expand on Sun Tzu's advice condensed into four main principles:

Ensure appropriate action

The quality of your action is more important than its magnitude. An appropriate action is one that is well timed and connected to the situation in precisely the way most favorable to you and the ends you are trying to achieve. To really understand the genius of this way of thinking, you need to constantly be aware of the relationship between your goal, your current position, and the way that your actions are relating to both.

When choosing goals, make sure that your actions are deliberate and strategic, which means that they connect intelligently to the result you desire. This may sound simple and pretty obvious, but the trouble is that in the "fog of war" (literal or figurative!) we can forget what we set out to do and get caught up in reacting to our opponent's moves.

In war, we are up against someone else's will and intentions, often times intentions that are deliberately opposed to our own. In life, too, we frequently encounter reality itself pushing back against what we want, thwarting our desires at every turn. Unless every action we take is directly contributing to the goal/effect we have consciously chosen, then we risk being tangled up in the will of personalities stronger than our own, or forces more powerful.

This process of goal setting and tackling smaller related tasks step by step is an iterative process, meaning it *must* adapt with changing circumstances. Modify and update your tactics. That doesn't mean letting go of the goal, but finding alternative paths to reach it. Ultimately, "appropriate action" is a moving target. The wise military leader and warrior knows that his success lies in regularly adjusting his aim.

See the world through your opponent's eyes

Sun Tzu calls for remarkable empathy and imagination in *The Art of War*, because it is only when we can truly understand the position and perspective of our opponent, that we can predict his behavior and ultimately defeat him.

In the more mundane world, your "enemy" can be anyone who is merely standing in the way, critiquing you, competing with you, or proving obstinate or unmoved. To convince and persuade others, to motivate them to your project, to soothe ruffled feathers, or even to conceal and manipulate, you need to understand the world as people see it. This requires the temporary suspension of your own point of view. It is an art to set aside our own strong feelings and preferences and consider the values, goals, thought processes, and interpretations of other people – which are often surprisingly different from our own!

Learn how your opponent collects and processes data, then subtly insert misleading information. Learn what they value, and you empower yourself to negotiate and trade to your advantage. Know what they know, and you can predict their thinking process and the plans it will produce – this allows you to prepare yourself against their actions. If you understand how others might perceive your plans and what strategies they might use to overcome or undermine them, then you can consciously build that into your strategy. All of this is what allows someone to be "a step ahead."

It's difficult to provide examples since this principle in action is by definition completely novel every time it occurs. However, imagine this: your company is hiring and, for your own reasons, you realize it would be great for them to hire a particular acquaintance you have in mind. However, in order to effectively steer the hiring manager's decision-making in your favor, you need to carefully set aside your own ideas and fully immerse yourself in their wishes for the position. Not only does this allow you to identify their perspective and directly "speak their language" so you can frame your desired candidate as a good choice, but it also allows you to carefully consider and pre-empt objections.

Master "perspective-switching"
We can take this "think like the enemy" principle even further and consider ourselves from the perspective of our opponents. What do we look like to them? In Sun Tzu's world, this all about defense, but in our world, it can also be a useful tool for truly thinking outside the box.

Real genius often reveals itself through its ability to self-reflect, correct, and adjust. One way of thinking of stupidity is to imagine that it's the same as being "stuck" – that is, *mentally* stuck in a single, narrow perspective, and not being able to step outside of that. This means that we are often surprised and undermined by factors we did not even know existed. We may, because of our own ego, cling too tightly to a plan that simply isn't working, and become blind to its obvious risks and downsides. In other words, we're behaving stupidly.

"Thinking like the enemy" is the genius of inverting this natural tendency and learning to look at ourselves with honest eyes. Review your strategy not as *you* would (since you have reason to be self-congratulatory and overlook flaws) but as a rival or enemy would. Only then will your most serious blind spots be fully revealed. This gives you the chance to more intelligently correct for them.

Simply ask how you may be exploited by others, ask what could go wrong, and ask what a harsh critic may notice about yourself that you, in either arrogance or blindness, might be tempted to ignore. This is not pessimism, but rather a mature, pragmatic mindset that values real knowledge and wisdom. It may take a little work to get your ego and fear out of the way, but remind yourself that a weakness acknowledged and managed is no longer a weakness.

Think holistically
Genius thinking is seldom linear.

Being able to see and understand a single isolated data point means little. Being able to see and understand two data points is a little better. Seeing and understanding three data points starts to paint a fuller picture. The more data points we add, the more dimensions we can include in our decision-making, and the more intelligent our working model of the world becomes. To think holistically is actually beyond intelligence – it starts to resemble wisdom.

In the West, we still hold onto a largely linear understanding of life, especially when thinking of intelligence itself. We imagine IQ as scalar (a quantity with magnitude only), and not as vector (a quantity that has a *direction*, i.e. a quantity embedded contextually in the world which is imbued with meaning and purpose). We imagine that if a smart man can solve a math problem in ten minutes, then a man who can solve it in five minutes must be twice as smart. Yet if we watched a ballerina complete a complicated routine twice as fast as normal, we would not consider her dance twice as beautiful, right?

The real world is composed of events that are more often like dance than they are like math.

Sun Tzu points to a subtler, Eastern view of intelligent conduct, which incorporates less linear qualities such as harmony, balance, and wisdom, and sees human intellect as much more than mere computation. Thinking holistically, we see a state of *continuity* that gives phenomena in a field relative value. We start to see large and complex interplays of interconnected phenomena, and not merely isolated actors tightly constrained under binary laws. Nature is seen as a living, constantly evolving entity, and our engagement with it is a matter of harmony just as much as it is a matter of truth. Sun Tzu, being the only non-Western entry on our list of exemplary geniuses, reminds us that sometimes genius is also about diplomacy and grace, and not just hard facts and the force of will.

As Confucius said, "Let the states of equilibrium and harmony exist in perfection, and a happy order will prevail throughout heaven and earth, and all things will be nourished and flourish."

Summary:

- **Sun Tzu's genius traits: holistic thinking, perspective switching, self-knowledge, cool-headedness, and restraint.**
- The warrior mindset shows us that genius is about more than art, science, or innovation. Sun Tzu teaches us tact, diplomacy, and the art of warfare that is ultimately fought and won in the mind.
- Sun Tzu encouraged knowledge of self and opponent, thoroughly considering alternative perspectives, thinking about "the big picture" as it unfolds in time, and favoring strategy over plain force.
- Sun Tzu's advice centers on being calm, contemplative, and prepared, never rushing or losing our tempers, and conducting ourselves at all times with grace and wisdom.
- **To be more like Sun Tzu, practice the art of (psychological) warfare and learn to master yourself. Be patient, contemplative and strategic in your thinking, and consider *all* dimensions of your situation, rather than just one or two aspects in the present.**

Chapter 7: Darwin's Golden Rule

Charles Darwin, the naturalist whose theories on evolution and the development of species had wide-ranging effects on scientific study that persist today, was not a genius. He wasn't especially good at math. He didn't have the quick-thinking skills often attributed to geniuses. Charlie Munger once said he thought that if Darwin attended Harvard in 1986, he probably would have graduated around the middle of the pack. Biologist E.O. Wilson estimated that Darwin's IQ would have been around 130 or so—high, but not quite the level (140) where the word "genius" starts getting mentioned.

Darwin was, however, relentless about learning. He devoured information about all the topics he was interested in pursuing. He hoarded facts and was hyper-diligent about taking notes. His ability to hold attention was legendary, and when it came to testing, his work ethic was tireless. Darwin's thinking was purposely slow because he was so fastidiously detail oriented. He believed that to have any authority on any topic one needed to develop deep expertise on it, and expertise doesn't happen overnight (or in a month, or in a year). The point is that Darwin is regarded as one of the ultimate examples of the importance of hard work and diligence in surpassing natural intelligence.

Darwin's uncommon talent

Darwin's method was so all-encompassing that he even gave deep attention to information that countered or challenged his own theories. This approach forms the backbone of his *golden rule* as he expressed it in his autobiography. The very basic guideline of Darwin's golden rule was to be more than just open to contradicting or opposing ideas—indeed, Darwin gave them his fullest attention:

"I had, also, during many years, followed a golden rule, namely, that whenever a published fact, a new observation or thought came across me, which was opposed to my general results, to make a memorandum of it without fail and at once; for I had found by experience that such facts and thoughts were far more apt to escape from memory than favorable ones."

Darwin completely immersed himself in evidence or explanations that went against his findings because he was aware that the human mind is inclined to dispose of those contrary views. If he didn't investigate them as fully as he could, he'd be likely to forget them, and that created mental dishonesty. Darwin knew that his own instinctual thinking could be a hindrance to finding the truth as much as it could help, and he established a way to ensure he wasn't missing out on any information.

Darwin handled all this conflicting information responsibly. He genuinely considered material that might have disproved his assertions, and took pains to fully absorb every single scenario, anomaly and exception to his theories. He didn't filter out information that didn't support his beliefs; he was utterly immune to confirmation bias. More than anything else, Darwin didn't want to be careless in finding the truth—he knew that a half-cocked assertion solely intended to persuade others without much thought was intellectually dishonest. His thorough method required more time and effort on his part, but he was committed.

Of course, the Darwinian Golden Rule calls back to intellectual honesty and the maxim "Strong opinions but held lightly." It assumes intellectual *humility*, as being unattached to any stances or theories and simply following the evidence.

Uniquely, Darwin forces a dialogue of skepticism back to himself, instead of to others in defensiveness. To himself, he would direct questions such as: *What do you know? Are you sure? Why are you sure? How can it be proved? What potential errors could you have made? Where is this conflicting view coming from and why?* As you can imagine, it takes quite a bit of self-discipline to constantly double-check yourself.

Darwin accurately realized that if you hold the belief that everyone *else* is wrong, you're in trouble.

What Darwin seemed to understand is that the biggest threats to our intellectual and cognitive rigor are often unconscious, personal and psychological, and nothing to do with the soundness of our arguments or the quality of our reasoning. In fact, you've probably encountered someone who cloaks their unconscious biases, assumptions and desires in neutral terms precisely to conceal what is really motivating their behavior. I.e. "it's other people who have irrational emotions and beliefs, but *I* only believe in the objective facts."

Truth > being right
Try this exercise yourself: think of something you deeply believe to be true—take your time with this, because it may be that your most pervasive belief is actually the one that is almost invisible to you. Now, imagine you are not

yourself, but a person who actually believes in precisely the opposite.

Play pretend for a moment, and *genuinely* try to occupy the other person's point of view. Imagine, if you like, that you are in a lively debate with yourself, as this other person. Really try to immerse yourself in this other worldview. What other priorities does that person have? What does the world look like to them? In what ways might they be right? As you debate yourself, don't worry about deciding who is correct. Simply watch what stories and narratives your brain throws up in the dialogue.

Internet activist Eli Pariser noticed how online search algorithms actually encourage our human tendency to grab hold of everything that confirms the beliefs we already hold, while quietly discounting or ignoring information that doesn't align with those beliefs. We set up a so-called "filter-bubble" around ourselves, where we are constantly exposed only to that material that we agree with. We are never challenged, never giving ourselves the opportunity to acknowledge the existence of diversity and difference. In the best case, we become naïve and sheltered; in the worst, we become radicalized with more and more extreme views, unable to imagine life outside our particular bubble.

The results are disastrous: a complete erosion of civic discourse, intellectual isolation, narcissism and self-centeredness, and a lack of everyday empathy, as well as the real distortion that comes with believing that the little world we create for ourselves is *the* world. When two people from mutually exclusive echo chambers encounter one another, the effect can be explosive.

We've already seen that for geniuses, broad is always better than narrow, and this applies here. We need to constantly be on guard for any stubbornness in ourselves, or any narrow, unchallenged convictions that are shutting us out of gaining a deeper, wider, and more nuanced vision of the great big world around us.

We can see how this ability to actively court the "other side" was instrumental to Darwin's success. Like both Einstein and Socrates, he was non-conventional, but only in the sense that he was willing to adjust his view if necessary, and never ruled out any avenue of inquiry (an attitude which is truthfully seldom in fashion!). Today, Darwin is credited with founding a completely paradigm-shifting theory that forever changed the way naturalists thought of the world and their place in it. He called into question many of the predominant religious and moral attitudes at the time, and there is evidence to suggest that he did so even when his findings contradicted his own assumptions. It's hard to imagine how Darwin could have done any of this without a deeper respect for truth, and an intellectual vigor that goes beyond personal bias.

At the time, the implications of Darwin's theories on natural selection made some of his contemporaries angry, and he was mocked for suggesting a view of the world that countered the dominant religious framework. Though the theory of evolution is now commonplace to us in the modern world, try to picture what it must have been like in Darwin's time, when the idea that man descended from ancestors that were not in fact human was as outlandish as suggesting they came from the moon.

Darwin was mocked and derided by many in his lifetime, but this didn't dampen his enthusiasm for continuing research he thought was important. Though most Victorian scientists at the time folded to public opinion and religious sentiment, not wanting to be unpopular or create a stir, Darwin didn't mind going against the grain, and his "golden rule" tells us how highly he must have thought of genuine intellectual enquiry, no matter where it took a person, and no matter how unpopular the findings were. Can we say the same for ourselves? Are we willing to risk pursuing an unpopular avenue of thought, or suspend the judgment of others in favor of coming to our own conclusions? It's easier said than done.

Consistency is often more valuable than brilliance

But intellectual honesty wasn't Darwin's only forte. He was also a remarkably patient man. Though Darwin was not considered particularly brilliant intellectually, it didn't matter, because he was abundantly blessed in the traits we've already identified as crucial to the genius's success. Darwin was intellectually honest, humble, methodical, disciplined, and an incredibly hard worker. Though he must have possessed considerable curiosity for the subject matter he pursued, and he was certainly a polymath like many of the others we'll consider in this book, Darwin's' life shows us that so much of what makes a brilliant person's life is not necessarily brilliant – it's just consistent.

Darwin didn't put together his many important works overnight. His work was a *life's work*, and took many, many years of diligent and focused effort. Like Socrates, he was unwilling to let bias and assumption derail or contaminate his efforts, and so made a concerted effort to weed out errors of thinking. And, like Socrates, he understood that the process towards knowledge takes time. If we are to piece together ideas that are sound and worth something, we often have to do so one step at a time, with many corrections along the way, and with as much stamina as we can manage.

Summary:

- **Darwin's Genius traits: Hard work and discipline, intellectual honesty, non-conventionality.**

- Darwin was a prolific naturalist whose works on natural selection, the descent of species and on evolution profoundly changed the scientific landscape, and set the stage for our current biological paradigm.

- Darwin was said to be a methodical, slow and exceedingly patient person who worked diligently on his efforts throughout his life. We can see the traits of hard work, self-discipline, consistency and resilience in his contributions to science. Though he was considered not to be a genius by many, this didn't matter, and he still managed to achieve enormous success that changed the world permanently.

- Darwin demonstrated a commitment to intellectual honesty, curiosity and humility by practicing what we called the golden rule. He would deliberately pay attention to material that countered his cherished beliefs, assumptions and expectations, knowing that his natural bias would be to ignore them.

- By courting alternative opinions and genuinely engaging with those that disagree with us, we weaken the hold of bias over our learning and gain deeper insight.

- Darwin's incredible life achievements would not have been possible were it not for his willingness to think outside the box, and to entertain ideas that were unconventional at the time.

- Darwin teaches us to be intellectually honest, and to follow the evidence, logic and facts wherever they take us, even if we have to abandon previously held beliefs, admit that we were mistaken, or come to conclusions that make us unpopular.

- **To follow Darwin, we can work hard to get out of our own "filter bubbles" and deliberately seek out information once in a while that contradicts with our pet beliefs. Switch your search engine or actively engage with people you ordinarily would have avoided. Get into the habit of asking yourself, "what am I not seeing here?"**

Chapter 8: Marie Curie and the Importance of Taking Risks

Marie Curie was a woman who routinely did what others could not. She was the first woman to earn a Ph.D. in France, and the first woman to win a Nobel prize – first in 1903 and then again in 1911. This also made her the first woman to earn two Nobel prizes, as well as the first person, man or woman, to earn two Nobel prizes in two different fields (physics and chemistry). In fact, to this day, she shares this accolade with only one other person in the world – Linus Pauling.

Marie Curie was born in 1867 in Poland as the fifth child of poor but intellectual parents, and she worked as a governess until the age of 24. She is most well-known for her work in radioactivity, and her discovery of two new elements, radium and polonium. These findings made possible the creation of x-ray techniques and novel cancer treatments options, the global impact of which can scarcely be calculated.

There is no doubt that humanity might not expect to encounter another mind like hers for many generations to come.

In 1995, her ashes were interred in the Pantheon in Paris, making her the first and only woman to receive such an honor. At the time, her ashes were still radioactive. While her contemporaries were becoming increasingly aware of the dangers of radioactive materials, Curie was known for using her bare hands and even pipetting by mouth. According to the biography, *Obsessive genius: The inner world of Marie Curie,* Curie even kept a bottle of pure radium salts next to her bed because she liked the "fairy-like glow" (Goldsmith, 2004).

Embrace the unknown

Curie is known to have said, "Nothing in life is to be feared. It is only to be understood."

Today, we live in a world where the concept of radioactive decay is an accepted part of science and happily taken as a given. But this was not the world Marie Curie lived in. The world she lived in contained various strange unknowns, and absolutely no hint as to how one might go about understanding them.

What has been sometimes described as recklessness is perhaps more accurately her *willingness to embrace and work with the unknown*. There are many gifted and intelligent scientists in the world who nevertheless stay firmly within the current bounds established by others. And then there are scientists like Marie Curie who tirelessly work to *extend* that range.

This requires an uncommon attitude, and Marie Curie herself frequently encountered other scientists (usually men) who told her that she had better stay within the bounds, rather than attempt to go outside them. At the first Nobel awards ceremony, the president of the Swedish Academy utterly diminished her towering accomplishment by quoting the Bible, saying "It is not good that man should be alone, I will make a helpmeet for him." Curie's own father, in referring to her groundbreaking discovery, said on his deathbed, "What a pity it is that this work has only theoretical interest."

In other words, Marie Curie encountered plenty of opposition, but it was not, as so many assumed, merely because she was a woman. Instead, the pushback she experienced was more fundamental; Curie was a woman who was truly willing and able to do something new. The resistance she faced was from those who were unable to accept her truly radical ideas (sadly for many male scientists at the time, the mere existence of a female scientist who knew better pushed the very limits of their imagination).

Nevertheless, Curie embraced the unknown. Her desire for knowledge and understanding far, far outstripped her concern for personal safety or reputation. *That* was the source of her fearlessness.

Today, many would shoehorn Curie into easy feminist narratives and claim that she was brave to fight against misogyny and oppression – in fact, Curie did much better than this, and refused to fight on those terms at all. She simply got on with the work she believed was important. She did not consider her womanhood a part of her achievement, nor an impediment to it. And neither should we. Rather, what remains is her "daring hypothesis." Her work stands on its own merits. Though often fatigued with the labors of her scientific investigations, she was wholly undeterred by other people's opposition and closed-mindedness.

Take a gamble on yourself
We talk oftenof confidence and self-esteem, but when it comes to living a truly innovative and pioneering life, it's about so much more than believing in yourself. It's about having the intellectual strength to take a risk based on your *convictions*. True scientists, ironically, often require a level of faith in their work that few around them can share during the work's initial stages.

Today, people happily print Marie Curie's face on stamps and curate exhibitions in her honor. Attractive actresses play her in blockbuster movies. Yet when Curie was alive, she was a humble, unassuming woman who did not enjoy the support or encouragement of others. Many people simply gave her husband the credit for the work she did, or made frequent digs at her looks, her intelligence, and her ability to mother her children.

Marie Curie didn't care, and gambled on herself anyway. The faith others lacked in her, she simply found for herself. When her husband died people continued to hold extremely low expectations of her, immediately assuming that she would claim her widow's pension, retire from lab work, and slink away quietly. Instead, she stayed on at the Sorbonne and eventually took over the lab herself. And yet throughout she was never arrogant or big-headed. Einstein himself said of her, "Marie Curie is, of all celebrated beings, the only one whom fame has not corrupted."

What stands out in Curie's career is her relative lack of interest in self-aggrandizement. She was not competitive, defensive, or intent on making a name for herself – all traits commonly associated with the other haughty intellectual heavyweights of her era.

It can be extremely difficult to follow your passions and interests when nobody around you can understand or validate them. But Curie derived justification from the work itself, and perhaps this allowed her to take what, to others, seemed like a radical risk. The rest of humanity can be grateful that she took this risk. Had Marie

Curie stayed home and dutifully fulfilled the smaller role that her society had carved out for her, life might look very different for all of us today.

Collaborate with others

Curie did not keep her research a secret, and openly shared her progress and findings with anyone who showed an interest – whether they were fellow scientists or not. In fact, when World War I broke out, Curie was eager to have her work applied, and oversaw the fitting of X-ray machines in ambulances, even driving these ambulances herself and directly assisting wounded soldiers. Considering how immensely rewarding it must have been to witness the genuine benefit to humanity her work had brought, we can start to imagine why Curie was so willing to collaborate and share her understanding far and wide.

The biggest impediment to fruitful collaboration is rather predictable: the ego.

Perhaps we hoard our knowledge because we unconsciously hope that it will give us an edge over others who we see as competition.

Perhaps we perceive in ourselves some lack that intellectual achievement will rectify, and feel threatened if that achievement should be shared and no longer attributed to us alone.

Perhaps we doubt the value of our work and are reluctant to share it until we're "ready" and it's perfect and complete.

Perhaps we feel unable to survive criticism, correction, or the discovery that we have been on the wrong path.

Perhaps we have bought into the illusion of the scientific genius as a brilliant, invulnerable lone wolf who only undermines himself by asking for help…

Whatever the specifics, it's worth being honest about any hangups that are keeping you working in isolation. Working with others provides valuable opportunities for improvement. Feedback is never a threat, but rather rocket fuel for your own growth and development. The achievements of others can aid your understanding, and that can only ever be a good thing.

Marie Curie was never discouraged or shamed by others, but she also never boasted or let bigheadedness get the better of her. Rather, her achievements came along with a refusal to focus on herself at all. Instead, she preferred to focus on her work and her effectiveness at making the world a better place. Working with others always amplifies your reach, and so Curie chose to do it whenever opportunity allowed.

If you find it difficult to keep fear and ego out of your own endeavors, if you have trouble believing in your vision when it feels like only you can see it, or if you find working with others either beneath you or too intimidating, then Marie Curie can teach you a lot about the value of humility and perseverance.

- Ask yourself what small risk you can take right now in your work or even personal life. Are you playing safe to appease others? To fit into a preconceived role? Seek out ways you may be unwittingly shying away from the unknown, and take a step towards it instead.
- Ask yourself what your ultimate source of validation really is. What would you continue to believe in and work towards, even if nobody else saw the value in your efforts?
- Ask whether there is something you are holding back from sharing with the world right now, for whatever reason. Could it be time to collaborate and seek feedback, even if it feels like your ideas are only half-baked at the moment?

You don't need to be a chemist or physicist to take inspiration from the way that Marie Curie lived her life. Though there are no more elements to discover (probably?) we will never run out of new horizons to push, or fresh corners of the unknown to explore, whatever that looks like in our world. If Marie Curie was anything, she was quietly assured of the value of tenacity. She said, "Life is not easy for any of us. But what of that? We must have perseverance and above all confidence in ourselves. We must believe that we are gifted for something, and that this thing, at whatever cost, must be attained."

Summary:

- **Marie Curie's genius traits: Tenacity, humbleness, the ability to take a gamble on her convictions and fully embrace the unknown, whether others could do the same or not.**
- Curie pushed diligently against constraints and resistance all her life. She made important and beneficial discoveries that benefited mankind, and pushed beyond intellectual limits all her life. Yet she remained modest, practical, and focused on her work and how she could continually improve.
- Her genius was characterized by a deep curiosity that completely dissolved any fear or self-doubt. She was proof that raw intellect paired with unshakeable principles can move mountains.
- **Be more like Marie Curie by deliberately taking a risk and gambling on your own convictions, even if only in a small way at first. Refuse to accept the limiting roles**

others assign to you, and persevere with what you know to be valuable.

Chapter 9: Rene Descartes and Starting "From Zero"

The Frenchman Rene Descartes is generally considered the founder of modern Western philosophy. It's a lofty title, but the magnitude of work he put forth in his life speaks for itself. Western European academics and philosophers at the time of his life (1596–1650) generally rushed to respond to his multitude of ideas, and that formed the backbone of the Enlightenment period of humanity.

What was his main contribution, for the purposes of this book, i.e. learning to think like a genius? Stubborn doubt and adhering to a simple mandate of the pursuit of truth. Oh, and not believing the thinkers who came before him.

Just because something was stated to be true did not mean it was because he was unable to either observe or reason it for himself. You can now imagine why his thoughts left other philosophers rushing to respond—because he upended literal centuries of thought.

And so eventually Descartes became known for his stances on doubt and not believing dogma for dogma's sake. He required proper examination and analysis; only from there could you be sure that you weren't building your knowledge on a house of cards.

The following words have sometimes also been used to describe his approach to thought: doubt, skepticism, distrust, and rationalism. All he wanted to do was discover and understand.

You could see this as not trusting in others, but rather, it was his way of gaining a sense of *certainty*. Without certainty in what we are saying through proof or experience, nothing can be taken as truth. And truth is all Descartes ever wanted.

Starting from zero

He suggests that it is pointless to claim that something is real or exists unless we first know how such a claim could be known as a justified true belief. But to say that our beliefs are justified, we have to be able to base them ultimately on a belief that is itself indubitable. Such a belief could then provide a firm foundation on which all subsequent beliefs are grounded and could thus be known as true. But how could we know that those beliefs are grounded and true? It seems like it could devolve into circular thinking, but those final beliefs must be based on what is provable or observable. Essentially, Descartes prompts a chain of asking "But how do you know?" until you can point to a direct experience or real evidence.

Can you think of a highly popular institution that this approach might conflict with, especially with events like the Spanish Inquisition burning people for heresy barely a century past? That's right: religion, which tends to be based on faith and the very absence of proof, which is an intentional aspect, not a shortcoming.

Although Descartes remained a committed Catholic throughout his life, you can imagine how controversial his writings were for the time. For reference, his contemporary Galileo Galilei was famously found guilty of heresy by the Catholic Church for his views on how the earth revolved around the sun—in 1633.

Ironically, Descartes' method of doubting was aimed at defending the Catholic faith and using reasoning and logic to confirm the truth of the religion. However, the Enlightenment marked an erosion of the Church's authority and influence, so perhaps Descartes had the opposite effect that he intended.

This brings us to where Descartes can help inform our life philosophy. He brings together elements of critical thinking, healthy skepticism, and doubt to ensure that we are seeing reality for what it is. Descartes can help us find the truth in everyday life just by shifting our perspective to one of slight doubt. It's not to say that you shouldn't be trusting, but simply reserving judgment at first is a powerful weapon in seeking happiness and making fulfilling decisions.

It's a life philosophy of caution, looking before you leap, and measured decisions. Some others might possess the philosophy of "never saying no" or *carpe diem* ("seize the day")—that's a different matter. You can still do those things, but first understand what the truth of the matter is.

In 1637, he published one of his most important works, including *Discours de la method*, but he published the main topic of this chapter on seeking absolute truth in 1641: *Meditations on First Philosophy*.

In it, Descartes discusses how we are able to check our beliefs against reality by essentially the first version of the scientific method. It consists of six meditations (we will only focus on the first three) about the proper method of philosophical reflection, proof, and the conclusions that can be drawn. Throughout,

Descartes insists that (1) we can claim to know only that for which we have justification and (2) we must judge our ideas using a method that guarantees that our ideas are correct and justified.

Here's something of a table of contents for *Meditations on First Philosophy*:

- Meditation 1: Use the Method of Doubt to rid himself of all beliefs that could be false.
- Meditation 2: Arrive at some beliefs that could not possibly be false and thus must be true.
- Meditation 3: Articulate criteria for true knowledge.
- Meditation 4: Prove that the mind is distinct from the body.
- Meditation 5: Prove the existence of God.
- Meditation 6: Prove the existence of the external, physical world.

We'll only cover the first three meditations; from the titles, it is probably apparent why this is the case. They are the meditations more directly concerned with finding truth and living life through a lens of critical thinking. The first three meditations work together sequentially through a sort of process of elimination. First, you eliminate falsehoods. Second, you sort through what's left. Third, you make a judgment based on what you find. It's a methodical way of thinking that, if applied correctly, allows you to understand the world better.

We'll go through each of the three meditations in detail.

Meditation 1

In his first *Meditation,* Descartes focuses on distinguishing between what is true and false.

To complicate matters, the fact that you have experienced something does not mean it is true. This is because of our senses, prejudices, biases, or perceptions. Everyone has their own version of truth, but that is not *the* truth. In order to test whether what we think we know is truly correct, Descartes suggests that we adopt a method that will avoid error by tracing what we know back to a foundation of indubitable beliefs. We have to challenge what we've always held to be true and doubt everything we know.

Such a radical flip might seem unreasonable, and Descartes certainly does not mean that we really should doubt everything in our lives, from our names to our heritage. He simply suggests that we should temporarily pretend that everything we know is questionable.

This is called *hypothetical doubt*, and we should hold such doubt regarding (1) the perceptions of our senses toward our experiences and (2) our reasoning abilities. As Descartes puts it,

> But inasmuch as reason already persuades me that I ought no less carefully to withhold my assent from matters which are not entirely certain and indubitable than from those which appear to me manifestly to be false, if I am able to find in each one some reason to doubt, this will suffice to justify my rejecting the whole. And for that end it will not be requisite that I should examine each in particular, which would be an endless undertaking; for owing to the fact that the destruction of the foundations of necessity brings with it the downfall of the rest of the edifice, I shall only in the first place attack those principles upon which all my former opinions rested.

Translation?

Descartes was the ultimate naysayer and contrarian. So he made the decision that he would no longer hold beliefs that had the slightest amount of doubt surrounding them. Logically, this would lead to knowledge and truth that was absolute. Practically speaking, this would be troublesome at best, but this was the essence of Descartes' famous method of doubt, the process of which will soon be articulated.

He recognized the impracticality of disavowing all the knowledge he had been taught and even observed (the sky is blue, right?), so he created broad categories of beliefs.

The first category consisted of beliefs that he had learned through his own senses. Surprisingly, he considered that the senses did not impart absolute truth. You can see that the sky is blue; everyone can observe the same thing, right? Not exactly.

> All that up to the present time I have accepted as most true and certain I have learned either from the senses or through the senses; but it is sometimes proved to me that these senses are deceptive, and it is wiser not to trust entirely to anything by which we have once been deceived... on many occasions I have in sleep been deceived by similar illusions, and in dwelling carefully on this reflection I see so manifestly that there are no certain indications by which we may clearly distinguish wakefulness from sleep that I am lost in astonishment.

We do not know that what we experience through our senses is true; at least, we are not certain of it. And we cannot tell when our senses are correctly reporting the way things really are and when they are not. So the best thing to do is to doubt whether any knowledge can be based on our sense experiences. Descartes didn't believe his senses, and this is best exemplified in his analysis of dreams.

In a nutshell, dreams lead to a certain type of experience, yet they do not represent reality. But it is often impossible to distinguish between dream experiences and waking, real-life experiences. Therefore, this experience is not a reliable source of truth and knowledge.

Descartes is not saying that we are merely dreaming all that we experience, nor is he saying that we cannot distinguish dreaming from being awake. His point is that we cannot be sure that what we experience as being real in the world is actually real.

Recall that the second portion of Descartes' method of doubt involved reason. This is to say that our reasoning abilities cannot always be trusted—this is a self-evident truth as we are always subject to cognitive biases, skewed perspectives, and simple errors. This is what is typically referred to as the *demon* problem, whereas earlier we had the *dream* problem.

> I shall then suppose, not that God who is supremely good and the fountain of truth, but some evil genius not less

> powerful than deceitful, has employed his whole energies in deceiving me; I shall consider that the heavens, the earth, colours, figures, sound, and all other external things are nought but the illusions and dreams of which this genius has availed himself in order to lay traps for my credulity; I shall consider myself as having no hands, no eyes, no flesh, no blood, nor any senses, yet falsely believing myself to possess all these things; I shall remain obstinately attached to this idea, and if by this means it is not in my power to arrive at the knowledge of any truth, I may at least do what is in my power and with firm purpose avoid giving credence to any false thing, or being imposed upon by this arch deceiver, however powerful and deceptive he may be.

Translation? We can't be sure that our reasoning abilities are trustworthy, honest, reliable, or correct. Descartes puts forth an argument to prove his point, just like before. If we think about a simple addition problem such as 2+3=5, then there are two possibilities about how we reach the answer. The first possibility is that our powers of reasoning are indeed reliable and sound, and thus we are calculating correctly.

The second possibility is that an evil demon from the depths of the earth is manipulating our brain, and we only come to the conclusion that 2+3=5 because the demon puts that idea in our minds. Here, we come to an answer via deception and a profound lack of correct reasoning.

Thus, we can only trust our sense of reasoning if we can ensure that the second possibility, and ones like it, are never occurring. But that's not possible. We can't ensure that our sense of reasoning is reliable or absolute truth—not by itself anyway.

This can be a highly disconcerting notion—to not be able to trust your own reasoning and thought processes. If you can't trust your senses or thoughts, then in what sense is your view of the world real or accurate? What, if anything, can provide the type of certainty that Descartes so desires? That is the very conundrum Descartes dealt with and strove to fix.

Meditation 2

Meditation 1 was about ridding oneself of the beliefs that could be false, most notably from our senses and from our mental reasoning. Meditation 2 follows on that thread and is about finding beliefs that are true no matter what.

How does one find these propositions if we cannot trust our senses or reasoning? It was only from those propositions that you could build knowledge of the world that was reliable and true—only by working from a base of truth could you have the chance of concluding truth.

Obviously, the point was clear that he must attempt to find universal truths that were without a doubt correct. From this particular line of thought sprung one of the most famous lines in all of Western philosophy. But first, his inner dialogue:

> But I was persuaded that there was nothing in all the world, that there was no heaven, no earth, that there were no minds, nor any bodies: was I not then likewise persuaded that I did not exist? Not at all; [surely] I myself did exist, since I persuaded myself of something. But there is some deceiver or other, very powerful and very cunning, who ever employs his ingenuity in deceiving me. Then without doubt I exist also if he deceives me, and let him deceive me as much as he will, he can never cause me to be nothing so long as I think that I am something. So that after having reflected well and carefully examined all things, we must come to the definite conclusion that this proposition, "I am, I exist," is necessarily true each time that I pronounce it, or that I mentally conceive it.

You may have guessed what's coming next. "*I think; therefore, I exist*"

In Latin, "*Cogito ergo sum.*"

This sprang from Descartes' argument for a universal truth, winding its way around the first meditation's two major roadblocks of not trusting senses and reasoning. The fact that *he* is being deceived by a demon is something in itself. If there is a deception, it must be acting upon something, and that something is Descartes himself. Thus, an undeniable truth must be that he exists.

Descartes realizes that he cannot question his own existence because he is a "thinking thing." Even if he doubts the senses and the body, he cannot doubt himself because of his thoughts. Even if we were to be deceived by an evil demon as to what we see and hear, if the thoughts are still there, we would still exist.

But to further expound on what *cogito ergo sum* actually proves, it doesn't mean that he exists as a person, a soul, or a body. It simply speaks to the limited scope that because he thinks, he exists, and thus the undeniable truth is only that he is a thing that thinks. Whatever thinks exists. Descartes thinks (albeit in a flawed way), and therefore he exists as a thinking thing.

It's almost the mental equivalent of a tongue twister. At this point, all Descartes has reasoned out is that he exists as a thinking being and there are no other things he knows for certain—not his name, his age, or the size of his bed.

Where can we go from here?

Meditation 3

> I am certain that I am a thinking thing; but do I not therefore likewise know what is required to render me certain of a truth? In this first knowledge, doubtless, there is nothing that gives me assurance of its truth except the clear and distinct perception of what I affirm, which would not indeed be sufficient to give me the assurance that what I say is true, if it could ever happen that anything I thus clearly and distinctly perceived should prove false; and accordingly it seems to me that I may now take as a general rule, that *all that is very clearly and distinctly apprehended is true.*

Translation? Well, Descartes sets a new standard for what could be considered true knowledge almost without us realizing it: "clearly and distinctly apprehended." But what does that mean?

When we see something *clearly*, then our vision is unblocked—we have a clear view of the object in question. It is not too far away, it is not blurry, it is not too dark to make it out, and so on. When we see something *distinctly*, we are able to differentiate the object from all other objects. If we see a button among a pile of similar buttons, we do not see it distinctly—we can easily confuse it for one of the other buttons nearby.

In other words, clear and distinct perceptions are defined by Descartes as those perceptions that are so self-evident that, while they are held in the mind, they cannot logically be doubted.

Examples of clear and distinct perceptions include the propositions "A=A" and "I exist." All knowledge, according to Descartes, is supposed to proceed from clear and distinct perceptions; no proposition is supposed to be judged as true unless it is perceived clearly and distinctly. Clear and distinct ideas are formally known as basic or self-justifying beliefs that Descartes hoped to use as foundations for his system of knowledge.

Consider the proposition that 2+3=5. We can have a clear understanding of the proposition (unobscured by other thoughts, with a clear understanding of the different parts of the proposition and how they fit together). Also, we aren't going to confuse it with some other proposition (e.g., that 2+3=6).

You might feel that there are some gaps left in this definition of absolutely true knowledge, but that will be addressed shortly.

From what we know in *Meditations on First Philosophy* thus far, our senses and reasoning are unreliable, and then the only thing we can know is that we ourselves are a thing that thinks (because we are thinking right now). This allows us to infer that, since *cogito ergo sum* is clear and distinct, clear and distinct propositions are the base of true knowledge. Or does it?

How can we say that clear and distinct propositions are indeed the most basic truth that exists? How can we be prevented from going down a further rabbit hole when we know that our most basic thoughts and senses are unreliable? How do we know the demon can't corrupt our thoughts on A=A?

This is where Descartes' devout Catholicism comes into play, and perhaps he deviates from his stance of everything requiring hard evidence and proof. God is the ultimate arbiter of truth and knowledge. This is also one of the most common critiques of *Meditations on First Philosophy*, because it seems to be contradictory to the very point of not trusting your own beliefs or thoughts.

> But when I considered any matter in arithmetic and geometry, that was very simple and easy, as, for example, that two

> and three added together make five, and things of this sort, did I not view them with at least sufficient clearness to warrant me in affirming their truth? Indeed, if I afterward judged that we ought to doubt of these things, it was for no other reason than because it occurred to me that a God might perhaps have given me such a nature as that I should be deceived, even respecting the matters that appeared to me the most evidently true...And in truth, as I have no ground for believing that Deity is deceitful, ...the ground of doubt that rests only on this supposition is very slight, and, so to speak, metaphysical. But, that I may be able wholly to remove it, I must inquire whether there is a God...and if I find that there is a God, I must examine likewise whether he can be a deceiver; for, *without the knowledge of these two truths, I do not see that I can ever be certain of anything.*

Translation? Descartes is worried that there might be a demon who has the power to confuse us or deceive us even about a very simple mathematical proposition, so there is the possibility that we only *think* we are being clear and distinct.

Certain propositions (*I doubt, I exist, I am a thinking thing*) are completely demon-proof.

However, he has said that even simple mathematical propositions are not. Thus, he uses God as a foil to keep the third meditation flowing. There are universal truths, espoused and approved by God, that we can find, and they are essentially categorized as clear and distinct. It's arbitrary and not overly helpful in determining categories, but this does logically flow.

Anything that is not clear and distinct is said to be not demon-proof; thus, it cannot be absolute truth.

Descartes the man
Now, we've spent a lot of time covering some of the ideas put forward by Descartes, but now let's turn to the man behind the ideas, and what we can say about the *quality* of his thinking style, beyond the content of his thinking. You can almost imagine Socrates and Descartes having a lively conversation – both of them seemed passionate about digging as deeply as they possibly could into the nature of things, beyond the limits of human understanding, beyond assumption, and, in Descartes' case, beyond doubt.

Descartes, like many other genius thinkers, wanted to *know*, and he wanted to have absolute, infallible knowledge that was unquestionable. He wanted something rock solid to build the rest of his philosophy on. In Descartes' thinking, we can see many of the genius traits we've discussed in their most potent form.

Curiosity – yes, plenty. In fact, so total was Descartes curiosity and inquisitiveness, that he wanted to peer into things as far as possible, he wanted *absolute* knowledge held with *absolute* certainty (or at least, he wanted to identify the method to finding it out).

Hard work and discipline? Yes, in buckets. A broad range of interests? Indeed. Descartes had a minor rank of nobility and enjoyed an enriched education at the Jesuit college at La Flèche, where he studied the classics, science, mathematics, metaphysics, music, poetry, acting, dancing, fencing and riding (he probably squeezed in quite a bit of Greek philosophy too). He later studied law. He invented analytic geometry and published many works on military architecture, metaphysics, and philosophy, and casually practiced medicine without charging his patients.

Descartes was a rigorous critical thinker and pursued what at the time was a rather non-orthodox route with dogged determinism and plenty of diligence. We cannot imagine Descartes achieving half of what he did without the help of these genius traits – in a way, Descartes formalized and put concepts to an intellectual approach that perfectly encapsulates the attitude held by many genius people. His work was to make plain a style of thought and an approach that perfectly characterizes not only the scientific method but the spirit of enquiry itself. He was a genius who's thinking focused on thinking – he was the ultimate metacognition!

How can we apply Descartes (admittedly stringent) standards to our own thinking in daily life? Let's look at the meditations again:

The first is that we use the method of doubt to get rid of all beliefs that could possibly be false. This is akin to throwing away any mental garbage that's accumulated in your mind. We don't have to completely throw away every conception of reality unless we have 100% irrefutable evidence for it, but we can commit to not holding too tightly onto beliefs and ideas that haven't strictly earnt their place. *How much of your current worldview is actually supported by cold hard evidence?* If we're honest, not much. You don't have to throw these ideas out; rather, be aware that they are provisional at best.

The second meditation asks us to positively hold onto only those beliefs that we know are true. This is likely to yield a very small subset of what we *think* we know. For Descartes, the very least he could say for certain was that he existed, because he was thinking. You, of course, don't have to settle for such slim pickings, and can concede a few more things in order to live practically in the world with necessarily limited knowledge. If we are scientists, we can commit (here's intellectual honesty again) to only holding beliefs that have a certain degree of evidence. If we are more practically minded, we may say we will only hold onto propositions and ideas that have demonstrated their value and function in our lives. In other words, is it true, or does it work?

In doing this, we are already practicing the third meditation, and articulating our criteria for true knowledge. Here, we can commit ourselves to being clear and concise in our definitions, and clearly recognizing and formulating the limits of our understanding and certainty.

Summary:

- **Descartes' genius traits: intellectual honesty, curiosity, diverse interests, non-conventional thinking.**
- French-born Rene Descartes is widely considered the father of Western philosophy, and greatly advanced many metaphysical concepts still in use today.
- Descartes genius was to start, like Socrates, from a point of complete ignorance, i.e. to begin in absolute doubt and work his way to true knowledge one step at a time, using rational and logical thought.
- In 1641 he published his *Meditations on First Philosophy*, the first three meditations of which are designed as exercises to help a person use the "method of doubt" to discard

false beliefs (meditation 1), find those beliefs that could not possible be false (meditation 2) and devise some rock-solid criteria for what constituted true knowledge (meditation 3).
- This approach is essentially an early form of the scientific method, as it outlines a path to true knowledge by removing everything that can be doubted and focusing on that which cannot logically be false, and therefore must be true. It's via this path that Descartes believed e built a sound philosophy.
- In the first meditation, we use hypothetical doubt to tease out truth from the inaccuracies of our own perceptions, as well as the flaws and limits of our reasoning faculties. We can practice this sentiment ourselves by reminding ourselves that we can always be wrong, and to take doubt as a starting point, rather than to make assumptions.
- Meditation 2 is about finding out what is true once all that is false is removed from the equation. This is where Descartes famous cogito ergo sum proposition comes about, explaining that at the very least, he knew he was in fact thinking, and that proved he existed.
- From this we are led to meditation 3, which discusses the criteria for universal knowledge as those things perceived clearly and distinctly.

- To take inspiration from Descartes, we needn't follow his complex philosophy in detail, but we can practice a kind of philosophical doubt, committing never to hold beliefs we know aren't true, and to have stringent standards for what we consider truth.

Chapter 10: Tesla and Edison: Two Paths to Success

For this chapter, we will have to consider *two* very prominent and successful people simply because it's so hard to talk about one without mentioning the other. Let's begin with Nikola Tesla, who many will agree embodies some of the world's fondest ideas of what it means to be an innovator. While many prominent figures from ancient history were certainly polymaths and had a wide range of interests, this could partly be explained by the fact that men of a certain class invariably did have varied, "classical" educations, and that it was not uncommon to expect such a gentleman to dabble in everything from art to politics to medicine.

However, true polymathy is less and less common in the modern world, as it becomes more complex. Tesla bucks the trend for specialism, though, and was known throughout his life for being interested in many areas, and a prolific and successful inventor with over 300 patents to his name. His most well-known contribution to science is his design of the alternating current electricity system, or AC electricity for short.

Edison – a teacher and rival

If this short biography sounds familiar to you, it's probably because it's very similar to the life story of Thomas Edison, who was granted a whopping 1093 patents for various inventions, including the phonograph, the alkaline storage battery, the typewriter, the "electric pen", the motion picture camera and yes, the lightbulb. As productive and industrious as his peer Tesla, he died leaving more than 3000 notebooks containing his prolific brainstorming over the course of his six decades of work.

Edison had no formal education at all, yet possessed one of history's most creative and out-of-the-box thinking styles ever devised. Though their approaches did differ, both Tesla and Edison shared a passion for lateral thinking, and both had a dogged determination to keep on pursuing the ideas they were interested in, no matter how many times they "failed."

Though Edison was certainly the most prolific and productive of the two, and worked hard all this life, arguably Tesla was the most inventive and novel in thought, challenging conventions in ways that are still noteworthy today.

In the late 1880s, two new but different electric power transmission systems were enjoying a moment of fierce competition, and three prominent scientists/manufacturers were engaged with what is now called "the war of the currents." On the one hand was high voltage alternating current (AC) and on the other was low voltage direct current (DC). The former was associated with arc lamp street lighting and the latter with newer, low voltage incandescent lighting used indoors.

On the side of DC was Edison, and on the side of AC was Tesla and George Westinghouse of General Electric. Edison had designed the world's first lightbulb in the late 1870s, dominating the market by around 1882. Enter young Serbian scientist Nikola Tesla, who immigrated to work with Edison on DC generators, but who also wanted to share his new idea for AC current devices. Fast forward to 1888 and Tesla has quit working for Edison and now has a few patents for his AC technology, which Edison claimed had no future. Tesla sold the patents to George Westinghouse, already a competitor of Edison's. Their success was immense.

Edison immediately embarked on a campaign to publicly discredit the superior seeming DC as dangerous. Though these antics were extreme (murderer William Kemmler was publicly executed using an AC generator heartily endorsed by Edison as deadly) Edison failed to convince the public away from AC technology, and Westinghouse ended up winning the right to supply the electricity to the enormous and much-lauded World's Fair in 1893. The war of the currents had been won, and Tesla, Westinghouse, and the new AC electrical systems were the champions.

Tesla's lesson: Pursue goals obliquely
What shall we make of this (admittedly brief) history of two powerful men vying for technological supremacy? Clearly, both Tesla and Edison were incredibly intelligent, productive men who both left indelible marks on the course of human history. Though Edison lost the current wars, nobody would argue that he hadn't achieved astronomical success in his hundreds of other discoveries, inventions and novel ideas.

In their own ways, both of these men demonstrate that trait so often associated with geniuses – that of being a jack of all trades. In the first chapter we discussed how having a broad range of interests is essential for a deeper, nuanced understanding of the world. We saw how Einstein was struck with the idea of $e=mc^2$ while playing the violin. It's not so much that the violin held some deep secrets about physics that could only be accessed by playing it. Rather, it's in the ability to mentally switch from one style of thought to another that seems to make a fertile ground for new, unexpected insights and creative ideas.

The very same thing happened to Tesla. He was reportedly out walking with a friend in Budapest in 1881, reciting poetry, when he was suddenly struck by a vision. At once, the young Tesla grabbed a stick and sketched out a crude diagram in the sand, all at once capturing the idea of a motor powered by two rotating magnetic fields arising from an alternating current. Several years later the vision became a reality.

Now, this isn't to say that poetry itself allowed Tesla to access some new understanding within himself. Rather, by using a completely different part of his brain, the recital of poetry seemed to allow Tesla's unconscious mind to relax and foment its own ideas. You've probably experienced this yourself whenever you suddenly have a really bright idea while taking a shower in the morning. Of course, diligent and focused effort are needed to bring visions to life, but sometimes, we can invite those novel visions by having an agility of mind, and a willingness to switch modes. Whether we do this by engaging with art, music, poetry, or spending time in nature (Bach is reported to have composed many of his greatest works after being inspired by listening to birds) is up to us.

Changing perspectives this way allows for novel insights and fresh takes on old problems.

Creativity stagnates when ideas don't move, or when we get trapped in one fixed way of working through a problem.

We can take a page out of Tesla's book by making liberal use of daydreaming, imaginative visualization, and simply taking plenty of free-form walks and breaks to let our unconscious mind do its thing. Step out of your comfort zone. When you're stumped on a math problem, give it a rest and spend the evening at a salsa class instead, for example. You may be surprised to find you have fresh eyes when you return to your work.

Work hard on a project but then set it aside for a while and flex another part of your brain – do a strenuous workout or pick up a paintbrush. Being a jack-of-all-trades means being a dabbler in many different areas, but for the purposes of this chapter, we can also think of it as being willing to switch things up often, to be creative, and to play fast and loose with the rules.

In this sense, thinking like a genius may mean taking creative breaks from "thinking" all together. Mental resources can get depleted, and our cognitive abilities can tire with effort just as surely as our muscles do when we exert ourselves physically. When we take strategic breaks and rest, however, we give ourselves the time to not only recuperate our mental faculties, but solidify memories and new concepts in our mind, so that we grasp and learn them more thoroughly.

Though there's a lot we can learn from Tesla regarding innovative thinking, persistence and productivity, one less appreciated lesson is that flashes of insight often take place in those moments *between* bouts of energetic study, during sleep and dreams, or in those quiet moments we take to deliberately let go of effort and let our unconscious mind take charge. If we remember to entertain a diverse set of interests, read widely, and have plenty of different hobbies, including non-cerebral ones, we give ourselves more opportunity to access other ways of thinking – ways that might hold the secret to our next big insight.

Edison's lesson: Pursue goals incrementally
What about Edison? If Tesla can teach us the power of switching tasks and taking breaks, what can Edison teach us? You might have wondered if there was a lesson in the fact that Edison, for all his genius, failed to see the value in his young protégé's ideas about AC current, and thus missed his chance to get involved with the next big thing from its inception. Geniuses are still human, and it might be that Edison's ego got in the way of him admitting that there was a better way.

Though Edison might have lacked in humility and intellectual honesty in this case, he certainly excelled in other genius traits we've identified, particularly in hard work and diligence over many years. It's true that Edison was an inventor, but it might be more realistic to say that novelty and innovation only played a small part in his work. He didn't invent the lightbulb, but rather *perfected* it, and he did so in a methodical, persistent way, going "back to the drawing board" again and again until he had fine-tuned the design after many iterations.

Edison was also a businessman, and was keenly involved in the manufacture and marketing of his inventions, not just their creation and design. While Tesla might have had flashes of insights while walking in the woods reciting poetry, Edison's approach was slower and steadier. He invented so many things because each new invention suggested a slightly different one. The phonograph (something to record sound) gave him the idea for a motion picture camera (something to record images) and so on.

This slow and plodding progress made by gradually improving on the previous step is something that seems trifling day to day, but the successes add up quickly. However, we can imagine that it's also what made it difficult for Edison to make the big conceptual leap from DC to AC, whereas it was more natural for Tesla to do so. Genius can advance and discover by *Eureka* moments and flashes of insight, or it can creep along with gradual manipulations and tweaks on the same subject banking progress as you go.

Alex Osborn, a thinker considered the father of brainstorming, was interested in this idea of small, cumulative manipulations of a subject, and described methods that may well have been used by Edison without him knowing it. A popular technique is called SCAMPER, and it's a mnemonic encapsulating the 7 different ways we can manipulate and handle data. If we hope to achieve even a fraction of the impressive success Edison found in his lifetime, we might do so by deliberately following the SCAMPER technique.

The mnemonic is as follows:

S – substitute

C – combine

A – adapt

M – magnify or modify

P – put to other use

E – eliminate

R – rearrange or reverse

Let's see how we can apply these manipulations to a topic productively, to generate new ideas and solutions, or simply to gradually improve on what already exists. Edison worked primarily with practical inventions and tools, but we can apply the same ways of thinking to more abstract ideas, too. Imagine you are launching a catering business and are just starting out with gathering new customers and refining your recipes.

You might look at a menu you've devised for an event and ask:

1. Can you **substitute** something? Perhaps there is an ingredient that is cheaper, more flavorful or easier to get hold of.
2. Can you **combine** what you have with something else? Maybe you can invest in some beautiful crockery and have an arm of the business that rents it out, too, or maybe you have a friend who is a master calligrapher, so you can offer handwritten menus as another service.
3. Can you **adapt** something to your subject? You already have a small garden at the back of your house – can you plant herbs there instead, so you can save on buying these?
4. Can you **magnify** anything to good effect? If you have one specialty, maybe you want to focus on that more – such as specializing in unique desserts.
5. Can you **modify** anything? Maybe you can offer you customers some kind of meal that's hard to find elsewhere, such as catering to special diets.
6. Can you **put things to another use**? Maybe the web domain you've already bought for

another project can be reworded to make a website for your catering business.
7. Can you **eliminate** something? Maybe you find it challenging and expensive to cater alcohol, so you decide to simply eliminate that from your menus entirely, and spare yourself the trouble.
8. Can you **rearrange** things? Maybe you notice that the online ordering process with clients is getting confusing, so you work on streamlining it, reordering the steps they go through to enlist your services.
9. What happens when you **reverse** things? You might wonder, after being in the business for a while, if you might make more profit by approaching the industry from an entirely new perspective – i.e. becoming a food wholesaler who sells to caterers. Maybe you would enjoy event management more, when you can sub-contract caterers without having to do the work yourself.

This catering example is merely to illustrate that we can always improve on things, even if the improvements seem small in the moment. Edison was famous for taking the art of trial and error to its extreme, and was known to literally try out hundreds of subtly different designs of his various inventions. Rather than generating some brand-new idea from scratch, Edison found his way to creative new ideas step by step, by modifying what already existed. Sometimes you might encounter people like this in your own life: when asked how they landed up in their successful fields, they tell you how they actually began on an entirely different path, but by degree wound up somewhere else entirely, through dozens of smaller steps.

Two very different kinds of genius
Edison was prolific, Tesla was innovative. Edison displayed amazing work ethic and determination over decades. Tesla had audacity and the drive to pursue something new and different. Both men, however, shared a passion for challenging convention, and they both had a wide and diverse set of interests. Both were non-conventional polymaths, Tesla driven by curiosity and Edison by the desire to constantly improve. We cannot imagine either of these great thinkers achieving what they did without these genius traits.

From Tesla we can learn to push and promote ourselves, even when we conflict with our superiors. Tesla left his employment under Edison because he wanted to grow. How many of us are contended to stay put where we are, as long as it's safe and comfortable? Tesla, however kept going. In his own way, Edison showed the same tendency, and, rather than settle with a "good enough" invention that more or less did the trick, he kept on improving it, not content until his inventions dominated the market and were sold everywhere.

Though few of us will match the achievements of these two titans of innovation and industry, we can certainly follow their lead in many areas.

Even when something is working, can we find a way to make it even better?

If we are stuck, can we take a step back and pause for a moment, to allow a completely fresh idea to emerge?

Do we have a rich variety of interests and skills, and are we constantly drawing on them as a resource?

If you allow yourself to be inspired by Edison and Tesla, use the SCAMPER technique often, and engage freely in many different interests (including rest!) then you will naturally find yourself a jack of all trades. Whether you favor Edison's approach or Tesla's, the overall lesson is that success belongs to those who are willing to pursue their own path with self-discipline, persistence and variety.

Summary:

- **Edison's genius traits: diverse interests, non-conventional thinking, hard work and self-discipline.**
- **Tesla's genius traits: curiosity, non-conventional thinking, intellectual honesty.**

- Edison and Tesla were two inventors engaged in the so-called current wars of the late 1800s. Tesla was an employee of Edison's, but became his rival when he took new ideas to a competitor, George Westinghouse, and found success there. While Edison had dominated the market with his DC powered systems, eventually the war was won by Tesla and the new AC electricity.
- Edison was a prolific and productive inventor who also manufactured and marketed his products across the country. His approach was to make gradual, iterative improvements to things that already existed, and he eventually had over 1000 patents to his name.
- Tesla's approach was slightly different, in that he was less prolific but more innovative, and able to seize the AC technology wave where Edison could not. Tesla was said to have had his greatest insights away from work, when he was relaxing or out walking.
- Both men were enormously successful individuals, and both possessed many genius traits, including determination, self-discipline, and the willingness to pursue their own interest even when it bucked conventions. Both men were also willing to keep pushing and challenging themselves to be better, rather than settling for mediocrity.

- **We can cultivate both Edison and Tesla's approaches into our own lives: firstly we can make sure we have a wide range of interests to switch between, and making sure we take regular breaks to refresh our minds and change our perspectives. Secondly, we can use the SCAMPER technique to manipulate our subject and arrive at new ideas and solutions step by step.**
- SCAMPER stands for substitute, combine, adapt, magnify or modify, put to other use, eliminate, and rearrange or reverse.

Chapter 11: Copernicus and Galileo: The Courage to Go Against the Grain

In today's world, most people admire non-conventional thinkers and rule-breakers, and we all understand that those mavericks and big thinkers who challenge assumptions today often end up being the ones to make astonishing breakthroughs tomorrow. But this attitude is a relatively modern one, and for most of human history, innovators and those who question things faced a most formidable challenge: the stubbornness of those around them.

Today, looking back in history, we have the benefit of hindsight, and can easily look at those who used to believe the earth was the center of the universe as foolish. But try to imagine what it was like for Galileo, that famous intellectual black sheep, who lived in a world where heliocentrism was so obvious only a heretic would argue against it. It would be the equivalent today of arguing that people could reverse their age or that it was possible for humans to photosynthesize.

What it takes to be different

To understand Galileo, we must understand Polish astronomer Nicolaus Copernicus, who was the very first to claim that the earth and indeed all the other planets orbit the sun in our solar system. Though educated and destined for a career in the church, Copernicus, like many others in his well-to-do class, also studied law, medicine, arts and astrology. For a time, Copernicus assisted his professors in making astrological predictions for others (astrology was far closer to astronomy than what we call astrology today), and gradually came to criticize the common geocentric, or Ptolemaic view.

The geocentric idea was that the universe was arranged in concentric spheres, with the earth smack bang in the middle, and everything rotating neatly in circles around it. Even simple observations, however, contradicted this idea, and many astronomers at the time simply couldn't explain why planets moved in unpredictable ways or even reversed their orbits sometimes.

Copernicus published several papers during his lifetime explaining his astronomical theories, and his book *On the Revolutions of Heavenly Bodies* was completed in 1543 and devoted to Pope Paul III. He compiled work on the earth's spin on its axis, ideas about orbits, the stars, eclipses, and other ground-breaking concepts that today are seen to be the true foundation of all astrology, cosmology, physics and mathematics. Though Copernicus would gain some fame around the world after his passing, at the time of his death in 1543, there were still several unresolved issues around the heliocentric theory, which posed as many new questions as it answered.

Galileo Galilei was born some years later in Italy in 1564, into a Christian world that still largely propounded geocentrism, despite the ground already covered. Through his efforts, the Copernican theory was extended and popularized in the early 17th century, with the help of other contemporaries like Johannes Kepler. But his work was plagued with near constant resistance from the church. The conflict was bitter and prolonged – the church had always held that God had created man at the center of the world, and to suggest otherwise was seen as sacrilege.

Whilst a man like Darwin managed to push through this resistance, Galileo lived in less progressive times and was publicly forced to recant his claims. Knowing what we know about intellectual honesty and freedom of inquiry, we can appreciate how severe a restriction this was to a man who only wanted to understand the truth.

Galileo is now known for championing the heliocentric view, but that was not his only achievement. He is also credited with the invention of the pendulum clock and the refracting telescope, for which he ground and polished his own lenses and experimented with magnification. Galileo used all the same principles of the scientific method we still use today, as well as a dash of Socratic questioning and the iterative process favored by inventors like Edison. He used observation and experiment, always looking to the data and what he observed – rather than starting with a fixed assumption and trying to make all observations fit that pre-conceived idea.

Using his telescopes, Galileo was able to see mountains and craters on distant planets. He investigated the planetary cycles and phases of Venus, and identified the moons around Jupiter, which are now called Galilean moons. He discovered that the milky way was in fact made of stars, and not just a mist of light, as was previously assumed.

It might tell us something interesting, however, that the work which we most associate with Galileo today was the work he was most villainized for in his own time. Galileo was eventually tried and convicted for heresy and was labelled an enemy of the Catholic church. He was threatened with burning at the sake, eventually took back his claims and lived under house arrest for the rest of his life. It was only much later with the work of Isaac Newton that the Copernican theory was gradually allowed to take hold in non-Catholic countries, and by the late 18th century, what had begun as wild conjecture was commonplace and universally accepted as true.

Incidentally, the Catholic church took a whopping 359 years to acknowledge that Galileo was in fact right, and eventually Pope John Paul II issued a formal apology in 1992 for the Vatican's wrongdoing. Though Galileo undoubtedly experienced extreme prejudice, many scientists both before and after him have felt the interference and opposition from superstition, irrationality, stubbornness and religious dogma. We have his persistence and brilliance to thank for the continuing advance of science, despite the interference from religious attack.

Geniuses are leaders, not followers

It's clear to see which of the genius traits we've identified are at work in both Copernicus and Galileo. In fact, the story of Galileo is most often used to demonstrate that if you are right, you are right, regardless of whether the entire world believes you are wrong. Sadly, many great genius thinkers are disparaged by their contemporaries simply because others have a hard time buying into the vision that the genius can see more clearly. It is only when the general consensus swings in the other direction, can popular opinion feel safe siding with what they were happy to denounce a few years before.

What is seen as exciting, novel and worthwhile to a genius may at the same time seem threatening, dangerous and pointless to a person who is more invested with the status quo. True geniuses throughout history, however, have always pushed on. We usually become aware of great scientists only *after* they've won awards and become celebrities, but if we had seen them before, we might have mistaken them for crackpots, crazies, deviants or delusional people who were wasting time. Galileo could never have achieved what he did if he allowed the church to put a complete end to his work.

Luckily for science, and for humanity as a whole, other great people were able to pick up Galileo's work where he left off, and carry the torch of enlightenment a little further, protecting it from being snuffed out by those who were fearful of change. Again, we see that the most successful, resilient and profound work was that done by people who were motivated only by the lust for learning, and the deep desire to understand. If Galileo had been driven purely by financial gain or the approval of his peers, he would have given up at the first criticism from the church – in fact he would never have had the courage to dream up a theory that contradicted it in the first place!

We can see that the trait most associated with both Galileo and Copernicus is non-conventionality, and a willingness to go against the grain. Galileo made observations and came to certain conclusions, and his intellectual honesty didn't allow him to pretend he didn't see what he saw. His insatiable curiosity meant that he couldn't simply abandon a promising field of inquiry just because it was unpopular (or rather, illegal) at the time. His intellectual honesty wouldn't allow him to falsify or distort his claims to make them more palatable, and he didn't mind making enemies if it meant he spoke the truth. Granted, Galileo eventually renounced his work under threat of death, but we can see this recanting as a mark against his society, and not a sign of his personal weakness.

What can we learn from these two great men, and all the other scientists, both famous and unknown, who worked tirelessly despite the lack of understanding and support from their society?

Navigating rejection
Human beings are social animals. We have all evolved in tribes and social groups that have left us with a deeply programmed belief that *acceptance = survival*. If we are accepted by the group, we are happy and well. If we are rejected, we fail. So, we try to follow the group and reject people who are outside our norms. It's this unspoken rule that keeps societies following

conventions and customs and adapting only slowly to changes in ways of thinking, even if they're for the better. What this means for the independent thinker, innovator or inventor is that they may encounter rejection, alienation and criticism on their path.

True, some scientists and great thinkers are celebrated, but this is often long after they've fought hard against the status quo and the resistance from doubters. We don't have to face persecution on the level that Galileo did, but we may nevertheless feel afraid of trying something new, and thinking out of the box, lest we rock the boat or invite criticism. How do we deal with this inevitable side effect of genius, non-conventional thinking?

Modern-day Japanese authors Ichiro Kishimi and Fumitake Koga wrote a book called *The Courage to be Disliked*. Inspired by their background in Western philosophy and Adlerian psychology, the two wanted to explore how we could be the people we wanted to be, without being unduly influenced and limited by the thoughts and opinions of others. Though Kishimi and Koga wrote primarily from a psychological perspective, we can see that they have powerful insights into how we can have more courage to pursue the paths we want to pursue, and be the kinds of people we want to be, whether that means completely upending the prevailing model of reality or simply putting your foot down with a pushy family member.

What do non-conventional people possess that others don't? How do they differ in their thought processes from all those people who are worried about offending others, about fitting in, about being praised or accepted, and so on? If we are honest with ourselves, we can probably identify times where we allowed social pressure, expectation or pride to get the better of us. Genius is not always about the amazing things you *can* think about; sometimes it's about having the strength of character to decide what you *won't* think about, be it the unfounded expectations of others or external pressures.

Resist Determinism

A key idea in Kishimi and Fumitake's book is learning to be empowered, and to take control over your own fate. Geniuses are people who act. They never passively accept things set out for them by others, but rather express their full agency, taking matters into their own hands and trying things out, without waiting for permission. Digging into this attitude a little, we can see that it comes from an absence of a belief in *determinism*.

Think about some unpleasant fact of life. One person looks at it, shrugs, and says, "ah well, that's the way it is, what are you going to do about it?" and leaves it alone. The other person looks at it, becomes curious, and starts to plan ways they can change it. They invent a solution. They design a tool to make the problem go away. They **change** the story or rally people around them to change the world somehow, to make it better. The first person has succumbed to a deterministic (and apathetic) outlook, whereas the second understands that they always have the power to act, to build, to decide.

So, in the case of Galileo and Copernicus, it didn't really matter that their theories were not well accepted. They did not see the pre-existing geocentric theory as written in stone, unable to be altered, in other words, a part of fate. Rather, they took charge, and acted in the ways they knew how. This fundamental difference in mindset is what powers all non-conventional thinking.

Just because you did it one way yesterday, it doesn't mean you have to do it the same way today.

Just because you failed once, doesn't mean you can't succeed later.

Just because you don't like how things are, it doesn't mean you can't change it.

In a way, this is the same mindset that underlies the "what if?" idea – the ability to look at reality and see it, but also see that it can be different, that it can change. So, what is your attitude to change? If you are like the geniuses in our book, you will be inspired, motivated, and irresistibly driven by change. You will look at the world and get excited about what *could* be. You see visions of things you could build or create or improve, and it excites you.

Own your work

Another big idea explored in the book is that each of us is only responsible for our own lives, and our own actions. In a way, non-conventionality comes with a hearty dose of independence. It is the ability to recognize that we are each individuals, and it's OK to think as we think. The idea is that we become empowered and strengthened on our path when we put our head down and do the work we need to do, without considering the work that *others* need to do. Their work is theirs, our is ours.

When you own your own work, you place your locus of control within yourself, and judge your efforts against your own values and principles. If we are anchored in our own mission, our own dreams and our own strengths, then we won't need to get approval and recognition from others; we already have it from ourselves. We cannot know what was in Galileo's mind as he was forced to renounce his findings, but we can assume that he wouldn't have persisted so long on a course he didn't believe in with every fiber of his being.

True freedom, independence and non-conventionality comes down, then, to the courage to pursue our path no matter what. Regardless of anything that's gone before, or of what people say, or what it costs, we pursue it. In fact, it's hard to imagine how many prominent scientists could have the stamina they do without some conviction that they were doing what *they* knew deep down was right.

Have faith in yourself

Though the big thinkers we have looked at in this book have been scientists and mathematicians, the truth is that even intelligent people are ultimately guided and driven by psychological, interpersonal influences. It's difficult to tell the difference between courage and faith in your convictions and just being confident in yourself and who you are. Though we associate genius with mental and intellectual superiority, the truth is that it takes emotional intelligence to trust ourselves, like ourselves, and have faith in who we are as people, no matter how different we may be.

When we succumb to peer pressure or twist ourselves out of shape because of other people's prejudices, expectations or judgments of us, we may do so because of a lack of self-esteem. It takes a lot of emotional strength and maturity to say, "I acknowledge other people's opinions of me, but I don't allow them to determine my fate. Only *I* determine my fate."

If we can relinquish a belief in a deterministic future we have no control over (i.e. fate), if we can own our own work and focus on that, leaving others to focus on their path, and if we can learn to be confident in the unique people we are, then we are well on the way to having the courage to go against the grain, and perhaps even have a chance at being truly revolutionary.

For some people, being a genius means being a celebrity, or a much-admired person that gets to enjoy being superior to everyone else. In fact, a genius must learn to walk alone, and to work on what they know is important even if it takes many years to convince others of its value – if indeed they ever convince anyone. Imagine a solo entrepreneur working for years on a mission that barely anyone understands, or a visionary who has a picture of what they want to create, even though everyone else thinks it's strange precisely because it doesn't look like anything they've seen before.

Whether you call it intellectual independence, free thinking, innovation, open-mindedness, creativity, non-conventionality or simply going against the grain, this character trait is perhaps one that is most difficult to cultivate in ourselves. The biggest impediment is our fear of being disliked, rejected or judged by others. If we can tackle this, and find a source of direction and purpose within, then we are far less vulnerable to the whims and opinions of others. If we want to live lives that resemble our intellectual heroes, one of the questions we must never stop asking is, "what do I value? What are my principles that I would follow *no matter what?*"

Summary:

- **Copernicus' and Galileo's genius traits: intellectual honesty and non-conventionality.**
- Copernicus was an astronomer who has been credited as being the first to put forward the idea of heliocentrism. It was Galileo who popularized and expanded these ideas after Copernicus' death, but Galileo also had many other accomplishments, including the invention of a telescope and the discovery of many great ideas in astronomy and mathematics.
- Galileo's ideas directly challenged the predominant religious worldview at the time, earning him scorn and even resulting in him being tried and convicted of heresy. He was forced to retract his statements under penalty of death.
- Galileo may have submitted to the church's persecution, but his ideas were revived by other scientists in non-Catholic countries, until eventually the heliocentric model was taken as fact by the end of the 18th century.
- Both Galileo and Copernicus possessed an uncommon originality and independence of thought, and pursued facts and evidence despite resistance from others. They both

achieved what they did because they were intellectually honest and wiling to pursue what they knew was right.
- We can follow in this spirit by understanding that sometimes success comes with willing to be disliked. If we can relinquish ideas of a deterministic fate, own our actions and our agency, and foster self-esteem for who we are, then we are less susceptible to the judgments and criticisms of others.
- **To be independent thinkers, we need to lower the value we give to social approval and increase the value we place on our own vision.**
- **To cultivate courage in ourselves, we can regularly check in with our own values and principles, and align with them always. Many geniuses are powered by an unflinching commitment to their own path. What is yours?**

Chapter 12: Alan Turing and the Power of Negative Thinking

Since the making of the 2014 film *The Imitation Game* with Benedict Cumberbatch, more people are now aware of not just the genius but also the heroism of British mathematician and code-breaker Alan Turing. Famous for cracking a German code device called the Enigma Machine during World War II, Turing's work also stood on its own merits and made important contributions to the burgeoning field of computer science. Today, his lifelong struggle to find acceptance as a homosexual man has also become an important part of his story.

Born in London, Turing was an outsider from the start, and quickly excluded due to his appearance, clumsiness, and shyness. Though he was not popular at school, he made great strides in math and physics, eventually finishing with a first-class honors from Cambridge, after which he slowly found his feet in the social world. He began work on his idea of a hypothetical "Turing Machine" after earning his masters, and gained his Ph.D. in 1938 in America before returning to the UK.

Just one year later, everything was turned upside down as Germany invaded Poland and the world went to war. The Enigma Machine resembled a typewriter and had already been created by Arthur Scherbius for the Germans during the first world war. It used several rotors to scramble text messages into ciphers to ensure secret communication. The possible combinations numbered *159 quintillion*, and the machine was reset every day, meaning the Germans could be forgiven for thinking they possessed the ability to generate unbreakable codes. Turing, along with the British Secret Intelligence Service's Code and Cypher School at Bletchley Park, would prove them wrong.

Eventually there would be 10,000 people working on the project as the war progressed, but Turing had been one of the original group of 24 Cambridge academics recruited for the task. Fellow Mathematician Peter Hilton, who worked with Turing in Hut 8 at Bletchley, said of him,

"It is a rare experience to meet an authentic genius. Those of us privileged to inhabit the world of scholarship are familiar with the intellectual stimulation furnished by talented colleagues. We can admire the ideas they share with us and are usually able to understand their source; we may even often believe that we ourselves could have created such concepts and originated such thoughts. However, the experience of sharing the intellectual life of a genius is entirely different; one realizes that one is in the presence of an intelligence, a sensibility of such profundity and originality that one is filled with wonder and excitement. Alan Turing was such a genius, and those, like myself, who had the astonishing and unexpected opportunity, created by the strange exigencies of the Second World War, to be able to count Turing as colleague and friend will never forget that experience, nor can we ever lose its immense benefit to us." ("Reminiscences of Bletchley Park" from *A Century of Mathematics in America, 2019)*

Now, our book does not have enough space to do justice to an explanation of *how* Turing managed to break the unbreakable code and crack the Enigma machine, but suffice it to say that Turing's work, like many of the other geniuses mentioned here, had significant historical impact. By gaining vital hidden intelligence, Turing's work allowed for certain strategic advantages for the Allies. Some believe the work shortened the war by up to four years, saving millions of lives and avoiding untold suffering.

Though Turing is now best known for his contribution to the war effort, he continued to develop computers and became fascinated with the idea of machines and their ability to replicate human thought. He was an active and prolific cryptoanalyst and logician, and even dabbled in pattern formation and mathematical biology. To this day, his "Turing Test" is a common benchmark for artificial intelligence, and refers to the ability of a machine to effectively fool another human that it is also human.

But what about that other part of Turing's life?

In 1952, he was arrested and charged with public indecency with unemployed 19-year-old Arnold Murray. Homosexuality being illegal in Britain at the time, Turing was offered the choice between prison or chemical castration. He chose the latter. Two years later, he committed suicide at the age of 42.

Just thirteen years later, Parliament passed The Sexual Offense Act which decriminalized homosexuality in Britain, and in 2013 Turing was given a posthumous royal pardon, later going on to receive further honors and awards for his life's contribution.

Computing the Uncomputable
Turing must have felt like his own life was a series of unsolvable problems, irreducible conflicts, and unfathomable circumstances. As a talented computer scientist working at the vanguard of his field, he understood the incredible power of algorithms to solve complex

problems. Today, algorithms are everywhere, and seem like a kind of magic that can solve any mathematical problem.

But, perhaps inspired by his own personal struggles, Turing knew that some problems could *never* be solved algorithmically, and that algorithms have their limits. He introduced the idea of "uncomputable" problems, i.e. those problems that reject any attempts made to solve them. They require an entirely different approach, in his case in particular a mathematical strategy based on what's called diagonalization. In his private life, Turing was an outsider and something of a contrarian. In his professional life, too, he made a name for himself by consistently seeking out alternative paths.

Turing's willingness to be unconventional and his oblique approaches to problem solving can be thought of as a kind of negative thinking. Here are some ideas for applying this kind of negative thinking in your own life:

Don't be afraid of unsolvable problems
Failure and difficulty certainly have an emotional component, but to Turing, his genius began with the plainly factual recognition that sometimes efforts in certain situations simply won't yield results. The first thing to do, in other words, is to carefully discern which problems are genuinely worth your effort, and which will simply waste time and demoralize you.

Granted, Turing's application of this principle was purely mathematical, but we can take inspiration from the general principle and apply it to all those circumstances that leave us feeling truly *stuck*. For example, if you really cannot make any headway in a challenging work environment, then it may be better to plan your escape rather than endlessly trying to fix things as they stand.

Again, this is not an emotional response; it is not about giving up, resigning, feeling like a failure, or getting angry. Rather, it's about clearly acknowledging the factual parameters of the situation you are working within. This means not getting hung up on what *should* be or what you wish was the case, but facing head-on what *is* the case, then calmly identifying the best course of action in which to invest your efforts.

Use constraints and limits to your own purpose
In mathematics, diagonalization is the theoretical equivalent of the man who learns to embrace and work within his constraints, rather than try to deny or solve them. It may seem counterintuitive, but limits can actually spur creativity. To convert this mathematical concept into a principle by which you can live your everyday life, consider what variables you may not be acknowledging whenever you're focused on all the things you can't do or currently lack.

For example, imagine you are preparing for a children's birthday party in 1 hour when you accidentally smash the birthday cake and realize that some of the games you planned won't be ready in time. These are constraints, but are they necessarily *problems*?

Thinking quick, you decide to create a brand-new dessert, "Ugly Cake", and set the kids up with a fun game of your own creation: they get to decorate a slice of broken cake with sweets and candy in outlandish ways, so that you can crown the winner of the Ugliest Cake Award. To your surprise, the kids love it so much that they request a rematch the following year. A difficult constraint in one area (the correct shape of the cake, the presence of official party games) actually opens you up to innovation in another area (i.e. fun, games and creativity).

Pay close attention and you may discover that whenever people are said to have thought "outside the box", what they have really done is found clever and unexpected ways to stay *inside* the box, so that others think, "Wow, I didn't know being in the box could be like this!"

Define success by what it ISN'T
Turing defined his problems by the solutions they rejected. He frequently found insight in the place neither he nor anyone else believed it to be found. You can do the same by defining your personal or professional success by what it isn't. In this way, you clarify your goals and priorities, and you end up learning a lot about boundaries, too.

To give an example of this principle in action, let's say you're a student trying to choose a suitable career for yourself. You may be pretty stumped trying to decide what you want to do, but you can always start by carefully considering what you absolutely *don't* want to do – then work backwards. If you know for certain you wouldn't be able to stand working in a cubicle, this tells you that you likely value more flexibility or space. Now you've arrived at a positive definition by exploring the negative.

Turing was a nonconformist, a rebel, and a contrarian, and his thinking bore the trademark of his character. By incorporating these negative thinking strategies into your own thinking, you can start to channel some of Turing's unexpected, upside-down brilliance to navigate your own challenges.

Summary:

- **Alan Turing's genius traits: Nonconformity, and the ability to understand and work creatively with limits, impossibilities, and problems.**
- Alan Turing was a master of "negative thinking" that allowed him to thrive within and despite constraints to completely triumph over so-called impossible problems.
- Despite enormous personal tragedy and an untimely death, Turing teaches us not to be afraid of unsolvable problems, but to turn

them to our advantage. He shows how to embrace limits and to not be defined by them. In his personal life he was a persecuted gay man who nevertheless received vindication after his death, becoming a hero and icon for the LGBTQ community and underdogs everywhere. Perhaps in his own way, he shows us that even some of life's most tragic problems may ultimately find their own kind of recognition.
- To be more like Alan Turing, embrace rather than avoid life's big, unsolvable problems, and learn to see the possibility and potential hiding in dilemmas and dead ends.

Chapter 13: Abraham Lincoln and his Team of Rivals

Recall Edison's attitude to "failure" – "I haven't failed. I've just found 10,000 ways that don't work."

When you are a scientist conducting an experiment, any outcome is valuable, because it adds to your understanding and knowledge, even if the result is not quite what you expected.

In this chapter, we'll be talking about a man who was known for his supreme political intelligence, leadership skills, and incredible statesmanship. Abraham Lincoln was perhaps not a genius in the conventional sense, but his cleverness lay in his ability to work with what he had, and to use diplomacy to make an impact. What Lincoln was particularly admired for was his habit of surrounding himself with people who actively disagreed with him.

Doris Kearns Goodwin has written a book exploring this genius approach of the famed former president, *Team of Rivals: The Political Genius of Abraham Lincoln*. The concepts that Goodwin outlines, however, are classic ones, and many others have understood the value of surrounding yourself with good people, and not necessarily just people who like and agree with you. It's essentially the same principle that Edison understood – we learn not by endless successes, but by failure, and challenge.

When elected to presidency, Lincoln assembled a rather surprising cabinet: the three men that he had beaten. These were "rivals" in the sense that they had competed fiercely with him, and were former political opponents who didn't share all his positions. But rather than letting his ego get the best of him and attempt to hide his competitors and critics out of sight, Lincoln did the opposite and deliberately sought to make use of their talents in government. In other words, the fact that they disagreed and were rivals didn't mean they couldn't be on a team and work towards the same goal – something perhaps unthinkable in the highly divisive modern American political landscape!

Lincoln's reasons were many. The first is that people who are actively competing with you (and coming close to besting you!) are going to be *good people*. Though they're competitors, they have valuable skills and talents, and Lincoln could see their strength even if it wasn't his own. Many geniuses toil away alone, on their own paths, perhaps fighting off competition. But for Lincoln, his genius lay in the fact that he could recognize the intelligence in others, and use that to his advantage, and indeed the advantage of the country he led.

"Keep your enemies close"

How many CEOs achieve their rank and then immediately work to get rid of all the people on their team they don't like? Why do they do this? Simple: they only want to hear what they already know, and they want a group of "yes men" to agree that their idea is best. They want people who won't challenge them, and if they're a little flattering, all the better.

But a person who never engages with different views, disagreement or challenge makes the same mistake as the person who cannot tolerate the first version of their invention "failing." It is not success that builds us up and makes us stronger, but rather challenge. We are not good leaders simply because we have found a group of people who will blindly follow us; rather, we develop real vision and strength when we can hold firm in our positions *because* we have properly considered the other positions.

The physicists, mathematicians and philosophers we've already discussed in this book may have been brilliant in a few areas, but many of them had disastrous personal lives, bad marriages, rocky relationships with friends and colleagues, or were irresponsible with money. Isaac newton was a virgin all his life and Adam Smith, famed economist, had his mother as a lifelong caregiver. All of this is to say that even genius has blind spots and weaknesses. It's a strength to see the strength in others, and work with it.

A great CEO realizes that they need all kinds of people on their team, with all different skills, including the skills that they themselves lack. A good leader understands that great things come from lively debate and negotiation, rather than simply having everyone agree all the time. A leader is just one person; but if they can synthesize the valid perspectives of *everyone*, they can rise against their own personal weaknesses, biases and ego. And if they make sure that their team includes those who will challenge them, so much the better, as this is the only way to let go of bad assumptions or ideas that aren't working anymore.

Lincoln's strategy worked extremely well for him. Though his political authority dissolved somewhat after his death, Lincoln's legacy continued on. His accomplishments are enormous: under his leadership the Union was defended and preserved, the principles of democracy were upheld and strengthened, and the practice of slavery was brought to an end. It's certain that Lincoln would not have been able to achieve all this in his term without his team of rivals, who in the end were not rivals at all, but allies and teachers.

Lincoln was a leader and visionary whose lasting attitude was one of unifying the nation under its highest principles and values. Lincoln understood that a nation that was united was strong – and they could be united even as they differed, and even as they disagreed. The way that he assembled his cabinet reflects the structure he envisioned for the entire country: democracy, respect for others and a unified goal towards one shared good were the guiding principles. Indeed, it's this spirit of democracy that fueled emancipation.

We can see Lincoln's commitment to working with his rivals as a form of practiced intellectual honesty. "Keeping your enemies close" can be seen as a way to keep yourself sharp, to make sure you're never getting lazy or egotistical, or making bad assumptions. On the other hand, Lincoln could be said to have followed something like Darwin's golden rule when he genuinely considered alternative perspectives, and entertained views other than his own. The idea is always that truth and cohesion are the highest good – and to this end Lincoln was always willing to place his own biases, his own pride and his own assumptions second.

This requires humility, honesty and the intellectual agility. It's a mark of strength to change your mind, and update your view when faced with compelling evidence to do so. If Lincoln hadn't possessed this genius trait, he would have never been the near-mythical and universally adored leader he is today, but simply another politician who was, in the end, mainly serving his own limited interests.

Many ways to be a genius

We seldom group accomplished political leaders in the same category as great thinkers like Einstein or Socrates, but perhaps we should. Lincoln possessed many of the traits we've identified as key to a genius's success. Endless patience, an iron will, shrewd political tactics, a sound economic mind, determination in the face of adversity, and perfect timing were all mandatory for the enormous tasks Lincoln was undertaking. Hard work and discipline were undoubtedly required in buckets.

Lincoln was also a polymath of a sort, and despite having very little formal education, had a wide range of varied interests, including science, literature, world history, geography, astronomy, poetry, music and even a little sewing. He is also the only president to hold a patent. Lincoln held many different job titles over the course of his life, including farmer, ferryboat crew, postmaster, store clerk and lawyer (not to mention president, of course).

Now, you're probably thinking that being a president is great and all, but what could a man like Lincoln teach more ordinary folks? Even if you never find yourself in a position of leadership, at work for example, and you never have what you'd call "rivals" or competitors like Edison and Tesla were, that doesn't mean you can't practice the same principles of intellectual honesty.

One great way to do this is to work with and take advantage of the skills of others. So many of us want to be right, to be the winners, and to dominate over our tasks as though they were dragons to be slayed. But the truth is that none of us is perfect, none of us has total control, and none of us in solely in charge. When we work with others, we can pool our resources, combine strengths and become better. When we work in isolation, we risk a too narrow focus.

So, true genius might be the intelligence to ask for help from just the right person at the right time. It might be the humility required to acknowledge who is more skilled than you, and finding a way to take advantage of that skill for the greater good. A little more of this attitude might have spared Edison from disregarding Tesla's ideas about AC current!

As with Darwin's golden rule, seek out opinions that counter your own. If you are criticized, listen genuinely to it and take it on board. Picture a new business owner who receives a poor review online from one of their very first clients. They're devastated, and their first instinct is to argue with them, and assume that person is attacking them. They could find a way to hide the review. Or, they could engage with the reviewer and genuinely ask their opinion. Humbly making changes, listening to feedback and even soliciting the advice of critics can have the opposite effect – many devoted fans of a company started out as disgruntled customers, but were later so impressed with how the owner managed their complaint, that they completely changed their view of them, and became their biggest advocates.

Was Lincoln non-conventional? We can see that he led his nation to make extraordinary advances and unified the national spirit. Perhaps compared to the others in this book, Lincoln was non-conventional but able to bring people around to his point of view, to wins hearts and minds, to make rousing speeches, and to inspire people to see his vision.

The power of mindset
We'll round off this book with a consideration of a genius trait that isn't on our original list. Nevertheless, this trait is one that allows all the others to come together beautifully, and allows any person to make the best of the genius traits they do already possess. Descartes was blisteringly intelligent. Socrates was ruthless. Einstein engaged in the "hard" sciences and Tesla and Edison were shrewd businessman.

But where Lincoln shines is in a separate skill set all together: the so-called "soft skills."

Lincoln had style. He was a brilliant speaker, a smart strategist, and knew how to work people. Yes, he possessed an inquiring mind, self-discipline and the courage to be non-conventional, but it was his attitude that allowed him to really share all these traits with the world. Firstly, Lincoln was a phenomenal communicator. In fact, his storytelling prowess was legendary, and he was widely known to be able to talk with anyone, about anything. His focus wasn't on conveying facts correctly or demonstrating his superiority; rather, he aimed to connect with his audience, whoever they were, using language to appeal to their higher natures.

Lincoln also inspired a certain respect because he was honest and forthright. People sensed his humility and responded to it, feeling as though they were listened to in his presence. You don't need to look far to find examples of people who are intelligent, skilled and technically right but who nevertheless annoy, insult or alienate people around them because they are unwilling to meet them halfway.

In this sense, the five genius traits we mentioned are almost useless if they are possessed by a person who is unable to relate meaningfully with others, and share those gifts. Lincoln possessed empathy and the ability to creatively imagine another person's world, addressing them most directly by appealing to their values and perspectives. This makes for good debate that really goes somewhere. Reportedly, Lincoln always responded calmly and respectfully, even when addressed by rude or angry politicians, and was sympathetic to all parties involved even as the Civil war raged on.

Soft skills are not merely something nice to have, or a kind of optional extra besides the harder skills of life. Consider again the five traits we've covered in this book:

- Insatiable curiosity
- Hard work and discipline
- Intellectual honesty
- Having a wide range of interests
- Non-conventionality

Perhaps you've already noticed something interesting: nowhere on the list is "extreme intelligence"! In fact, these traits could also be called attitudes or mindsets, and consist of behaviors that we can consciously develop in ourselves, whether we consider ourselves gifted intellectually or not.

Thus, a person with moderate intelligence but all the "soft skills" that include a great mindset and work ethic, will always perform better than someone with all the natural talent in the world, who nevertheless wastes that talent.

In the beginning of this book, we thought about what it really means to be a genius, and conjured up the image of the effortless, slightly arrogant smarty-pants who is always right. But could it be that what makes a real genius is actually all the *other* stuff? Granted, being smart helps, but perhaps it doesn't get very far unless it's also accompanied by good habits and the right attitude.

Lincoln's talent for empathy and communication didn't make him a pushover. He was still an excellent critical thinker, who could see issues from many sides and entertain all sorts of opposing political positions, thinking out of the box precisely because he was so good at understanding everything that was *in* the box! This is an attitude that takes self-confidence and a strong moral code.

He was resilient, and never gave up trying to achieve his dreams, even though he failed the first few times he ran for the House of Representatives. It took a full 26 years after that for him to achieve the office of president – and he worked hard throughout that time. We cannot imagine anyone having that kind of stamina and dedication unless they had the *attitude* of resilience. This bears repeating: it's not a question of raw talent, or being good enough, but a question of attitude.

The secret ingredient: humanity

One of Lincoln's greatest and most lasting achievements was his famous Gettysburg address, a speech which still resonates through history with those familiar first lines recalling the Declaration of Independence, "Four score and seven years ago..." The speech was surprisingly short at just ten sentences long, but it was honest, direct and potent. It was given during the American Civil War in 1863, at Gettysburg, Pennsylvania, at the Soldiers' National Cemetery. It followed a few months after the Union armies defeated the Confederacy at the Battle of Gettysburg, and honored those soldiers who had died in defense of the principle that all men are created equal.

The latter half of the speech explains, regarding these fallen soldiers, *"The world will little note, nor long remember what we say here, but it can never forget what they did here. It is for us the living, rather, to be dedicated here to the unfinished work which they who fought here have thus far so nobly advanced. It is rather for us to be here dedicated to the great task remaining before us—that from these honored dead we take increased devotion to that cause for which they gave the last full measure of devotion—that we here highly resolve that these dead shall not have died in vain—that this nation, under God, shall have a new birth of freedom—and that government of the people, by the people, for the people, shall not perish from the earth.*

In this speech, Lincoln not only shares his own powerful source of motivation – the drive to do what is right, to fight for justice, to defend democracy and honor those who have made the same sacrifice – but he also shows us just how easily he could put such grand concepts into simple words. Spectators reported being awed at the speech, delivered plainly and powerfully, and some reports say that the crowd was hushed into a stunned silence afterwards.

Lincoln was not only able to perceive and reach for a better vision of the world, but he was also able to powerfully communicate this to others, so they could share in this vision with him. He speaks as a leader, without self-aggrandizing and without complicated speech. Here, we see the powerful root of Lincoln's attitude – his moral convictions. Here was a man who could summon up self-discipline, hard work and resilience because he knew deep down that he was fighting for something genuinely worthy. And isn't this the defining feature of all great people?

In the end, Lincoln was a simple boy born in a log cabin in Kentucky, and received no more than a year and a half of formal education. Yet, he became the president of the country and, more than that, one of the country's greatest presidents of all time. Surely, there's a lot more to his success than simply being smart. Lincoln won success because of a combination of natural ability, hard work, perseverance and a deep conviction for pursuing not just fact, but *truth*.

Summary:

- **Lincoln's genius traits: intellectual honesty, morality, non-conventionality, and skills such as empathy and communication.**
- Lincoln had little formal education and had an ordinary background, but was someone who possessed all the skills we associated with genius. He was most talented, perhaps, at working with the genius of others.
- After he was elected president, Lincoln surprised everyone by appointing his "team of rivals" consisting of men the men he had beaten in the election, and who often disagreed with him. But with this team, he was able to achieve the enormous accomplishments he is still known for today.
- Like Darwin, Lincoln understood that success and learning come from challenge and the courage to consider alternate and conflicting viewpoints. Lincoln's cabinet also allowed him to make use of people's diverse talents.
- Lincoln was also, unlike many in this book, a master at soft skills such as empathy, communication, and the ability to tap into a strong moral code of ethics to power his goals.

- The 5 genius traits already covered are enhanced and transmitted more effectively when combined with these soft skills, as Lincoln demonstrates. Under his leadership, the Civil war ended with emancipation and the end of slavery, as well as a new and unified national spirit that defined the democratic principles of the country going forward.
- **To be like Lincoln, we need to know how to ask for help, to work with others, to engage our critics and competition strategically, and to take even our enemies as our best teachers.**
- **Lincoln also teaches us the power of connecting not only with our own moral compass, but connecting with other people via their values and principles, to be better communicators and more effective leaders.**

www.ingramcontent.com/pod-product-compliance
Lightning Source LLC
Chambersburg PA
CBHW060605080526
44585CB00013B/693